Pivot!™

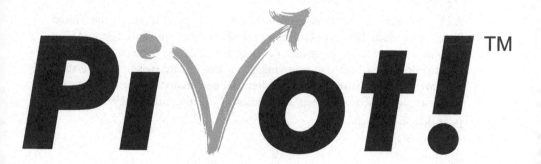

Pivot!™

THREE BIG QUESTIONS THAT...

- REFRAME YOUR PERSPECTIVE,
- MAXIMIZE YOUR POTENTIAL,
- AND IMPROVE YOUR LIFE

BY SAM SILVERSTEIN

AUTHOR OF *I AM ACCOUNTABLE* AND *NO MORE EXCUSES*

Published and distributed by:
SOUND WISDOM
P.O. Box 310
Shippensburg, PA 17257-0310
717-530-2122

info@soundwisdom.com

www.soundwisdom.com

Cover/jacket design by Eileen Rockwell

ISBN 13 TP: 978-1-64095-223-2

ISBN 13 eBook: 978-1-64095-224-9

For Worldwide Distribution, Printed in the U.S.A.

2 3 4 5 6 7 8 / 24 23 22 21

To my grandparents, Sarah and Samuel Silverstein and Celia and Max Wortsman. Your lives serve as perfect examples of what being able to Pivot is all about.

Acknowledgments

THREE WEEKS after I sent the manuscript of my most recent book to my publisher, David Wildasin, I called him to discuss a book idea that I had. This was right after the start of lockdowns and quarantine from COVID-19. I shared with him my vision for a book that was not only relevant at any time, but particularly important now. David immediately got behind the project, and within 60 days he had the finished manuscript in his hands. David and the entire team at Sound Wisdom made this book a reality for you, my readers, in an amazingly short amount of time. They work tirelessly to make sure that my projects look great and offer great values. I cannot thank the entire Sound Wisdom team enough for everything they do on my behalf.

I also need to acknowledge my personal editor, Cara Wordsmith, Ltd. Their involvement on this project, like so many others we have worked on together, is a critical factor in taking my ideas, concepts, and beliefs and creating the best possible finished product. Thank you.

And to you, my readers, thank you for all of the wonderful feedback and support you provide. You continue to inspire me to dig deeper, grow bigger, and deliver books that impact all of our lives.

Contents

Chapter 1

What Does It Mean to Pivot?

PIVOTING **IS WHAT HAPPENS** when you see one door closing…and you choose to respond, not by beating on the old door, but by closely examining your core beliefs and then using them to identify a brand-new door, one that opens you up to a whole new world of possibility. Each and every challenge you encounter is your opportunity to Pivot by diving deep into what you believe about yourself, about other people, and about the challenges you face in life.

There is something fascinating I have noticed about human beings, something that is either tragic or miraculous: people attain their full potential only when they come face to face with a challenge, a difficulty, or a low point in their life. The obstacle could be a life-threatening situation, or it could be something as simple as not making the high school basketball team. Regardless of the form it takes, adversity causes some people to descend into a spiral of negativity and inspires others to rise up and become their very best. What we believe determines whether we experience a challenge as a tragedy or a miracle.

Maybe you have noticed this as well. When things come too easily for people, they often become complacent. They tend to drift away from their potential. Yet once they come face to face with major adversity, some people rise to the occasion. Some people achieve truly remarkable things and make truly extraordinary contributions. This comes about as a result of a specific way of thinking, a way of thinking that can be learned. Human beings attain their full potential by asking themselves certain powerful questions about what they believe.

Pivoting is what happens when you see one door closing… and you choose to respond, not by beating on the old door, but by closely examining your core beliefs and then using them to identify a brand-new door, one that opens you up to a whole new world of possibility. Each and every challenge you encounter is your opportunity to Pivot by diving deep into what you believe about yourself, about other people, and about the challenges you face in life.

Everyone I have ever looked up to as a role model has, at one point or another, adopted this habit of Pivoting by *looking more closely at the* core *beliefs that drive them to be their best*…and becoming stronger people as a result. They have asked themselves big questions in response to adversity, and they have used the answers to those questions to *discover what they believe at the deepest level of their being, apply those core beliefs to the challenges they face, and transform themselves and the world in which they live.* I believe that pattern—the pattern of choosing to identify both our critical core beliefs and our untapped strengths—holds true in the lives of all good role models.

> "There are uses to adversity, and they don't reveal themselves until tested. Whether it's serious illness, financial hardship, or the simple constraint of parents who speak limited English, difficulty can tap unexpected strengths."
> —Sonia Sotomayor

This book came about as the result of me asking myself what I now call the Three Big Questions. At first, I did not even realize I *was* writing a book. I had just finished a major project, and I was looking to take a break. But this message had been given to me to share, and I found myself compelled to start writing. The book you are now reading ended up more or less writing itself...after I formalized the Three Big Questions and started putting them into practice in my own life.

You will be learning a lot more about these Three Big Questions as we move forward together in these pages. Before we examine them, though, I would like to share a couple of my favorite examples of what Pivoting looks like in action so you can begin to get a clearer understanding of the stakes for which we are all playing.

The Year of Living Differently

The pandemic of 2020 changed so many things for people everywhere. Suddenly we all had major challenges in our lives to deal with—challenges we never imagined that we would have to address. That made 2020 a hotbed of adversity…and it also made 2020 a seemingly limitless source of opportunities to Pivot. 2020 was the year I put into practice this new structure for thinking, believing, and living differently.

One of the amazing things that happened during this period took place on the Internet. An actor by the name of John Krasinski—you may know of him from his work on the television show *The Office* and films like *A Quiet Place*—had a great idea. Krasinski's idea, like so many great ideas, was a simple one. It came in response to the tidal waves of terrible news that we all found ourselves having to deal with on a daily basis in early 2020.

Krasinski's idea was as follows: What if there were a YouTube show, accessible to anyone who could find an Internet connection, that focused solely on good news? (Even posing this question, by the way, serves as an example of how we can all use what I call the Second Big Question for Pivoting…but I am getting ahead of myself.)

The whole concept and execution of Krasinski's online show, *SGN* (a.k.a. *Some Good News*), was a master class in Pivoting that came in direct response to the daunting challenges of the global COVID-19 pandemic. Instead of beating on a door he did not like—the relentlessly negative news of the day being circulated through just about every media outlet—Krasinski decided to open another door and walk through it. His show had a huge positive impact on untold millions of people. In every episode, he found ways to focus our attention on inspiring examples of human beings finding creative, empowering ways to respond to challenges and adversity—because when you get right down to it, that is what human beings do best. So the show's very existence is the first example of Pivoting that I would like to share with you.

Let me tell you about my favorite episode of the program, which includes my second example, an extremely important one. It was posted on May 3, 2020. Krasinski reached out to high school and collegiate members of the world's Class of 2020—most of whose in-person graduation ceremonies had been canceled due to the coronavirus—and did something marvelous. He conducted a virtual graduation ceremony for them. In preparation for that ceremony, Krasinski asked the soon-to-be-graduates to send in questions that they would want to pose to an (unidentified) commencement speaker. As it turned out, he chose four great questions and matched them up with answers from four stellar commencement speakers. The one speaker whose remarks I want to share with you as I open this book is none other than the incomparable Oprah Winfrey. Oprah was asked to respond to this question:

> Think about a moment in your life that felt like a low point at the time it happened, but actually changed everything for you. What was that moment and how did it affect you?

Here is what Oprah had to say to Amanda Gorman, the 2020 graduate—and newly named youth poet laureate of the United States of America—who had posed that question:

> There have been several times in my life, Amanda, when things didn't go the way I wanted. This one event, though, was the most influential in my life.... I was twenty-two. I got this big job working in television as an anchor on the local news program in Baltimore, and I was placed with an older gentleman who didn't want me to be there—but I didn't know that. I came in for the fall of 1976, and by April 1, 1977, I'm being called in by the bosses and told that I am no longer going to be needed on the news. I thought it was an April Fool's joke! Anyway, I get demoted. I am humiliated. I am embarrassed. But what they did was, instead of firing me, they put me on the local talk show. And the day I did my very first talk show, I felt like I had come home to myself. I believe that failure is an opportunity to move yourself in a different direction. I believe it gets better—because you've learned the lessons.[1]

What Oprah was describing is another great example of Pivoting, and I want you to remember it because we will be coming back to it and evaluating it much more closely in the next chapter. For now, though, just imagine yourself in her situation. You win—and then lose—the job of your dreams. What then? Do you beat on the closed door? (That is the tragedy.) Or do you find a new door to open and walk through? (That is the miracle.)

My aim is to show you how to make Pivoting a daily, hourly, and minute-by-minute reality in your life by using the Three Big Questions to transform your way of thinking and believing when challenges, big and small, show up in your life.[2] It is in our response to these challenges that our true potential as human beings lies. It is when we Pivot that we capitalize on our greatest opportunities. Challenges are going to come, whether we want them to or not. The three questions I will be sharing with you in this book will help you to navigate virtually any challenge in your life in a positive and empowering way.

If that possibility is of interest to you...please keep reading.

> "Think about a moment in your life that felt like a low point at the time it happened, but actually changed everything for you. What was that moment and how did it affect you?" —Amanda Gorman

Notes

1. *Some Good News,* episode 6, "SGN Graduation with Oprah, Steven Spielberg, Jon Stewart, and Malala," hosted by John Krasinski, aired May 3, 2020, *YouTube,* http://www.youtube.com/watch?v=IweS2CPSnbI.

2. This also applies when there are *not* major challenges in your life. As a matter of fact, the right way of thinking may prevent certain challenges from showing up in the first place.

Chapter 2

The Flight to a New Place

HERE IS HOW THE SIMPLE, powerful tool I now call the Three Big Questions presented itself to me. I was flying to Atlanta; a major client was bringing me in to speak to their team. The flight was smooth. My mind, however, was restless and bumpy.

Normally, a flight to Atlanta like the one I was on would be a cause for relaxation and pleasant anticipation for me. Atlanta, after all, is where I am from. My mother lives there, as well as my brother and his family. Because I was arriving in the city a couple days ahead of my speaking engagement, I had the opportunity to spend some time with them. On any other day, this trip would be a matter of getting to the airport on time, catching my flight without incident, getting some work done or maybe reading a book during the journey, and thinking about what I was planning to do with my mom and brother. But this particular flight found me preoccupied and more than a little uneasy, all because of a discussion I had had a few days before with Craig, the client whose team I would be speaking to.

That discussion had started out as a routine call for me, and I am sure it sounded like a fairly straightforward call to Craig, too. There was really nothing memorable about the content of the call as it unfolded. It is part of my process to reach out to the person who hired me several weeks or even months before the event and discuss the goals of the program. I had had my normal pre-event call, but for some reason this time I felt an additional check-in call before the event would be important.

I really cannot explain why what Craig said to me near the end of that call made me feel as unsettled and introspective as it did. He said: "Be sure you give my people three things to think about when this program is over."

I have received this kind of request many times before—and often during the very type of call I was having with Craig. It was a request I had fulfilled successfully, and without any particular internal struggle, every single time it had arisen in the past. And yet this time, Craig's seemingly simple instruction set my head buzzing from the moment I had settled into my seat on the airplane.

At this stage in my career, my content on accountability, being an accountable leader, and building accountable organizations is well developed—which meant there were way more than three good points in my program already!

It should have been a simple matter for me to accept that and just move on. But for some reason, something deep inside me was pushing back against that. It was as though some part of me knew that in order to fulfill Craig's request at the highest possible level of quality, I needed to rethink everything.

All through the flight, the discussion with Craig kept stirring in my mind, burning a hole in my awareness and preventing me from focusing on anything else. What three important things would I be sharing?

As we began our descent into Atlanta, I began to think about doing something that I would not have considered possible: redesigning my program from scratch. Not only did I think about that question, I prayed on it. As the plane landed, I still had not received an answer to my prayer or found any clarity on the questions that simply would not go away: What can I share with this audience that will absolutely rock their world? What can I give them that will allow them to change their thinking so dramatically that they will be able to do exactly what they need to do in their organization and in their life?

I got off the plane and made my way to my mom's home. But I knew that something big lay ahead of me. I had not just taken a flight to Atlanta; I had taken a flight to a whole new chapter of my life. I knew I was about to change the way I thought about everything and the way Craig's team thought about everything. I just did not yet know *how* I was going to do that.

Why Bother Changing the Way We Think?

Usually, when we run into a challenge, we focus most of our effort on changing what we *do*…and we make little or no effort to change the way we think. Yet the power of thinking far outstrips the effects of doing. It is only when we change the way we think that we will change what we do.

If you fix only the way you do something, but you are still thinking things through in a way that does not support your best self or the best potential of other people, you will never secure and sustain meaningful improvements in what you do, your relationships will suffer, and you will descend into a negative spiral whenever you encounter a challenge. On the other hand, if you fix the way you think and you connect with the fountain of personal wisdom that I call your Source, you will *automatically* upgrade the way you do things—and improve all of your relationships. Your Source—which is the set of unique lessons, examples, and reference points that clarify your beliefs and instantly direct you toward your best self—will enable you to turn even the gravest challenges into opportunities.

> Your Source is the set of unique lessons, examples, and reference points that clarify your beliefs and instantly direct you toward your best self.

Now, I realize that the points I have been sharing with you may seem vague and even a little unworkable at first. So let me make them specific and practical by connecting them to the powerful example we looked at in Chapter 1. What made it possible for Oprah Winfrey to transform the experience of losing her dream job into a new opportunity—a new door she could walk through that would summon the very best from her?

She had to do a deep dive into what she really believed about the challenge she faced. That deep dive enabled her to Pivot.

Make no mistake: There is an art to transforming what you believe. I can assure you that Oprah got an early opportunity to practice and master that art when her boss sat her down and told her that she would no longer be sitting at that anchor desk in Baltimore. I guarantee you that Oprah found a way to re-evaluate her belief structure about what that experience *meant*. I am positive that she found a way to connect to what she really believed about the challenge she found herself faced with and about the appropriate response to that challenge.

Initially, she believed that she had been humiliated and embarrassed. *She did not linger very long in that belief.* She went back to her Source. She exercised conscious control over her belief system, which is the amazing thing our Source *always* empowers us to do as human beings…and she redefined what she believed the experience of losing her dream job *meant.*

She no longer believed that losing that assignment meant that she had been publicly humiliated and embarrassed. She now believed that the "demotion" she had received meant she had a chance to give something of herself, to contribute, to take a new and unexpected situation and give it her very best effort, even though it was not what she thought she wanted. When she walked through that door and resolved to do her new job at the highest possible level of quality, that was when Oprah Pivoted. Pivoting transformed her worst career setback into her greatest opportunity to contribute.

Let me emphasize a critical point. The reason the new position was a success was that Oprah gave it her very best. The reason Oprah gave this new situation her very best was that she believed (and still does) that you always give your very best effort in everything you do. Her actions followed her belief. Action *always* follows belief!

> Action always follows belief!

Imagine what would have happened if she had *not* changed her belief system about the challenge she faced! Imagine what the outcome would have been if she had been bitter and resentful and had simply gone through the motions in her new assignment. She would not have been open to the incredible opportunity that had just come her way. She would not have done a good job. And she would have wasted precious time, attention, and energy trying to become a better local news anchor! What a loss that would have been for everyone!

This is not another book about doing. There are plenty of those already out there. This is a book about changing what you think. It is about discovering what you really believe and connecting your actions to those core beliefs. It is about how you think now and how you *could* be thinking. This is a book about becoming the best you can possibly be for yourself, for your family, for your organization, for your community, and for the larger world…by learning to do a deep dive into what you believe about yourself, other people, and the life with which you have been blessed. This book shows you how to take full control of what you think, once and for all…by tapping into your Source.

Your Source always draws you toward the best person you are capable of being. You might be skeptical that you can locate or take advantage of your Source, or perhaps you are even skeptical that you have such a thing. But you do. And locating it so that you can unlock its extraordinary positive impact on yourself and others is easier than you might imagine.

> Your Source always draws you toward the best person you are capable of being.

What you learn in the pages that follow will allow you to be the best, most accountable *you* possible. That means becoming the best person possible, becoming the best leader possible, building the best organization possible, and building the best world possible—by building accountable relationships. In your ability to Pivot lies the key to your best future, both personally and organizationally. In your ability to Pivot lies the key to accountability and excellence.

> "Excellence is never an accident. It is always the result of high intention, sincere effort, and intelligent execution; it represents the wise choice of many alternatives—choice, not chance, determines your destiny." —Aristotle

Meanwhile, Back in Atlanta

So there I am in Atlanta. I am spending time with my mom and my brother, but I still cannot stop thinking about the upcoming program with Craig's team. I am trying to be a good son and a good brother, trying to focus on being with them, but this nagging question of what three things I can share with that group will not go away. To put it bluntly: I am distracted.

Then, the day before the program, late in the afternoon, this crazy thing happens. The outline of a whole new program hits me like a freight train. Suddenly, I knew what the three things were. The answer flooded into my head, and I knew instantly that it was what Craig and his team needed to hear. Not only that—I realized it was what *everyone* needed to hear.

The night before the program, I found myself staring at a legal pad, with a pen in my hand, wondering, "Am I really going to write a brand-new program the day before the event?"

Yes, I really was. So for the rest of the evening, I scribbled out a brand-new speech, rehearsed it, and prepared to present it the next day. The funny thing is that I only really needed to go through the new material once to totally "own it." Somehow, this content was already in me.

I have been a professional speaker for nearly three decades. I have never once even considered writing a speech the night before an event. I might refine a few things. I would certainly *review* my ideas the night before a program. But prior to that evening I spent with that legal pad in my hotel room, I would never, ever have even dreamed of structuring a whole new program the night before I was supposed to go out in front of a group. However, in this case I felt I had to, and here is why.

The day before that program, it hit me that there are three powerful questions that we must each ask and answer for ourselves, regardless of whatever struggle is necessary for us to reach the answers. If we take on these questions, we will be able to get control of what we think, any time we want. That is how powerful the act of generating the answers to these three questions is. If I had not shared those questions with my client, I would not have been delivering my very best. And that is something I knew I had to do.

Once we answer these three questions for ourselves, we can then live those answers consistently. We can return to the questions whenever we face a challenge, do a deep dive into what we really believe, and walk through a new open door. We can Pivot!

I will close this chapter by letting you know that that legal pad, covered with scribblings, was all I needed as I made my way in to deliver my speech to Craig's team. The speech I gave that day not only transformed Craig's team, but it also transformed *me*. The Three Big Questions have the potential to transform you, too. Here are the questions you and I will be looking at closely together in this book:

- What do I believe?
- What do I focus on?
- What am I committed to?

Don't stop now! Keep going!

PiVot!™

Use the Pivot! Journal provided on page 143, get out your own notebook and a pen, or, if you prefer, open a word processing document. Whichever format you choose, the document you are now creating is to be devoted expressly to the exercises you will be completing as you make your way through this book. This is your *Pivot!* Journal.

Take a few minutes to write these questions in your *Pivot!* Journal. Do not try to answer them yet. Just write down the questions and think about them.

- What do I believe?
- What do I focus on?
- What am I committed to?

Chapter 3

Larry's Dilemma

A WHILE BACK, I was giving a presentation to a group of business leaders. This was a dinner with key members of an organization, held the evening before a program I was going to deliver to the entire organization. After dinner, as I addressed the assembled group of leaders, I made the point—a critical one that I make in every such gathering—that truly accountable leaders make and fulfill commitments based on what they believe and value most strongly.

As I usually did, I put special emphasis on the word *believe*. Most of the people nodded in solemn agreement with what I had said. A man who looked confused was sitting halfway down the right side of the long table around which we were gathered. His name tag said "Larry." I saw his hand go up. He had something he wanted to ask me.

Larry asked, "Sam, what if you don't know what you believe?"

This was a question that had not occurred to me before. I had always operated from the assumption that leaders *knew* what they believed, or could easily identify their most important beliefs about themselves, their organizations, and the world at large. I had always assumed that leaders worked from that foundation. This, as it turns out, was an erroneous assumption.

Larry had taken me by surprise. He was being completely honest. For a moment, I was not certain how to respond to that honesty. What I ended up saying to him was, "It's essential that you take the time to *figure out* what you believe and why you believe it." And I left him with the thought that this was something important that he needed to figure out.

That was true enough, but looking back I wish I had given Larry a deeper and more helpful answer. Today, I would challenge him to take the time to step back, examine his own life story closely, and follow the process that I will be sharing with you in this chapter to *identify* the core beliefs that supported him and could help him make good decisions. (Larry, if you are reading this, please accept my apology for the late reply!)

I would also assure Larry that by taking the time to ask himself, "What do I believe, and why do I believe it?," he could learn to define, act on, and defend a unique personal belief system that fits him like a glove and constantly draws him toward his own fullest potential.

I believe that each of us must deal with the moment when we realize we do not yet have a coherent belief structure and acknowledge that we are, for as long as we allow that state of affairs to continue, operating from a position of limited integrity and limited potential. I believe each of us, at some point, faces Larry's Dilemma.

Most people, I am sad to say, never take action to resolve that dilemma—and their lives and the lives of those around them suffer for it. Here are some signs that you may be facing Larry's Dilemma:

- Making decisions in extremely critical situations is difficult for you, and you hesitate, postpone decisions, reverse decisions frequently, and spend a lot of time second-guessing yourself. **When you know what you believe and why you believe it, decisions on important issues happen once and relatively quickly. And after you have made decisions you do not feel anxious or wonder if you made the right call, because you know what you believe.**

- In answer to these questions: "What do you believe about yourself?" "What do you believe about people?" and "What do you believe about the world you live in?" you either struggle…or you come up with different answers at different times for different situations. It is even possible that you present one set of beliefs to one person and an entirely different set of beliefs to someone else. Or your answer could vary depending on what is at stake, how much money is involved, or who is affected by the outcome. **When you know what you believe and why you believe it, the answers to these questions are always the same, no matter what circumstances you face.**

- You encounter crisis after crisis, because your beliefs are shifting constantly and your decisions follow no clear pattern. There is no consistency, which means that there are unacceptable levels of stress and chaos in your life. **When you know what you believe and why you believe it, your decisions are consistent and there is a clear direction to the choices you make in life, big or small.**

This is not to say that all your decisions are easy. But when you know what you believe, the *foundation* of your decision-making is solid, and relying on that foundation does not make you doubt yourself. To the contrary, your belief system makes you more sure of yourself. This is because your core beliefs—the beliefs that truly support you and others—align with both your decisions and your actions...and when you put them to work, they give you more and more evidence over time that making a decision based on your beliefs is the right thing for you to do. As a result, you do not waste time or energy worrying about whether your decisions are going to be popular. You do not even consider compromising on something that lines up with your core beliefs. You put a stake in the ground. You defend your beliefs. Period. Even when you face a situation that features challenging conditions, your core beliefs allow you to make a decision and move forward confidently.

Larry's Dilemma must be confronted directly. You must have the bravery to acknowledge your situation—that you do not yet know what you believe—and then figure out what you *do* believe. You cannot expect to Pivot if you do not know what your core beliefs are. On the other hand, once you *do* know what your core beliefs are, you can Pivot by ensuring that your actions align with your beliefs.

> "The pressure of adversity does not affect the mind of the brave man.... Such a mind is more powerful than external circumstances." —Lucius Annaeus Seneca

Case in Point: Decision-Making in a Crisis

President John F. Kennedy's decision-making process during the 13-day Cuban Missile Crisis of 1962 is often cited in business schools (and elsewhere) as a model of effective leadership in response to an unexpected, and deeply dangerous, situation. What is less commonly recognized about this episode, though, is the degree to which Kennedy's personal belief system drove his decision-making.

That belief system was as follows: Human life is a human right. Kennedy once famously observed, "Is not peace, in the last analysis, basically a matter of human rights—the right to live out our lives without fear of devastation—the right to breathe air as nature provided it—the right of future generations to a healthy existence?"[1]

Powerful words. Inspiring words. But plenty of people speak powerful and inspiring words without backing them up with action… which means they do not really believe the words that come out of their mouths. Politicians are particularly vulnerable to this syndrome: they may say one thing, but they often engage in actions that show a complete break with the beliefs they claim to hold. Was Kennedy among them? How do we know for certain that his beliefs were more than mere rhetoric, more than a decision to speak words that sound good in a given situation?

By his actions.

You and I may encounter any number of opportunities to Pivot during the course of our lives, but we are unlikely to find ourselves looking at one with higher stakes than the one that confronted President Kennedy during the Cuban Missile Crisis. Early in the crisis, Kennedy asked for an estimate of the total casualties if he followed his senior military staff's recommendation and launched an air assault on the island of Cuba, where the Russians were in the process of constructing secret nuclear launch sites. The answer that came back stunned the president. "Pierre," he said to his press secretary, Pierre Salinger, "Do you realize that if I make a mistake in this crisis 200 million people are going to get killed?"[2]

That, for Kennedy, was an unacceptable outcome. So in keeping with the belief that human life is a human right, Kennedy totally redesigned White House decision-making, because he knew full well that the decision-making model he had been working with would produce an outcome that violated his beliefs. And he was not willing to let that happen. As a recent article in the *Harvard Business Review* put it:

> [O]n the morning of October 15, 1962, President Kennedy and his team learn that the Soviets are placing nuclear-armed missiles in Cuba—missiles that a few minutes after being fired would kill eighty million Americans.
>
> That very morning, top military brass insist on an immediate and massive military strike to take out the missiles. But…instead of debating only the one plan, they follow [a] new approach, which calls for exploring options. As the new process unfolds, Kennedy instructs his brother to lead a thorough deliberation of the two alternatives…. Frank discussions ensue. "There was no rank, and in fact we did not even have a chairman…the conversations were completely uninhibited," Robert

Kennedy would later recall…. In this way, the groups are able to probe decisions and surface pros and cons. Two days later, the group presents the fully developed alternatives to President Kennedy, who chooses to pursue the blockade. The blockade is successful, and prevents a nuclear confrontation with the Soviet Union.[3]

Kennedy's decision—his *action*—was in alignment with a specific belief about people, namely that human life is a human right. Defending that belief meant pushing back against the Joint Chiefs of Staff, who unanimously recommended a missile strike. Kennedy pushed back. As a result of that decision, that action, we know what he believed.

At some point in his life (I do not know when), John F. Kennedy made a decision about what he believed about the value of human life, and he also made a decision about the lengths he was willing to go in defense of that belief. And thank goodness he did.

I believe we all eventually face such a moment of truth. The question is whether we will take the time to respond authentically to it. Many of us do not take that time. Many of us stumble through life for years or even decades, wasting precious time making decisions that do not align with any belief system. All too often, those decisions lead to crisis.

Get Clear on What You Believe

Write this sentence in your *Pivot!* Journal:

BIG QUESTION NUMBER ONE: **WHAT DO I BELIEVE?**

Once you have done that, begin in earnest by completing the exercises you will find below. Take as much time as you need for these exercises.

Exercise 1: Your Source Experience

A Source Experience is an event, good or bad, that taught you an important lesson about life. From that lesson you gained clarity about what does and does not work for you, and you are able to trace what does work back to its origin.

That origin you track down could be a person who served as a mentor or guide to whom you kept coming back, or even a book that you returned to over and over again, such as the Torah, the New Testament, the Quran, the *I Ching*, or even *The Hitchhiker's Guide to the Galaxy*.

Your task for this first, vitally important exercise is to *identify three powerful Source Experiences in your life...and put them into words.*

Keep them private if you wish; it may make it easier for you to write if you begin from the premise that only you will read these entries.

Something counts as a Source Experience for you if:

- You remember, and can put into written words, at least one clear lesson arising from the Source Experience. Multiple lessons from a given Source Experience are fine, but as you work on this exercise, try to identify one in particular that you feel certain has been, or should be, important to you as you move forward in life.

- The lesson you draw from the Source Experience respects the rights of others when followed.

- Each Source Experience you write about in your *Pivot!* Journal points to a different lesson.

Before you commit the details of your Source Experiences to writing, read the four examples that follow.

Example #1: *Rediscovering the Golden Rule*

Although Bill did not consider himself a Christian, when I asked him to identify a Source Experience that matched all three of the criteria you just read, he told me that the question had taken him to an unexpected place. He said that he instantly knew what he wanted to start writing about: a passage from the Gospels of the New Testament.

Bill told me, "I am not strongly focused on Christian belief or practice. But the question was, 'What was an experience that led to a single clear lesson that I felt was important to me in life and that respected the rights of others?' That, for me, instantly came down to the Golden Rule of the Gospels: 'Do unto others as you would have them do unto you.'"

An excerpt from Bill's *Pivot!* Journal for this exercise reads:

> I chose the Golden Rule because it perfectly summarizes the operating principle I aspire to, and because it most obviously meets the criteria you set down about respecting the rights of other people. I'm sure there are other great teachings that are relevant from the Gospels and from other sources that could qualify as Source Experiences, but this is the one Bible passage I remember from my youth when my parents took me to church. I cannot pretend that it is something I always live by, but I can say that when I notice that I have failed to live by it, I want to look closely at what led to the choices that I made that took me off track.

Example #2: *Finding Meaning in Adversity*

When I asked Jennifer to complete this written exercise, she wanted to know if a college instructor who had had a major impact on her would qualify. There was apparently a Russian literature teacher from her sophomore year of college who had left a positive impression on her. I told her that if the instructor was someone who had led her to at least one clear, powerful life lesson—a lesson that she could put into words and that respected the rights of other people—then he would qualify. She struggled with that—and ultimately decided to write, not about the instructor, but about one of the authors he had assigned to her: Leo Tolstoy.

An excerpt from Jennifer's *Pivot!* Journal for this exercise reads:

One powerful and enduring lesson I took from Tolstoy, a lesson I keep coming back to, is that even in hardship and difficulty, I can find meaning and purpose and learning and growth. I can get clearer on who I am meant to be as a person, and I can do that in response to the challenges I encounter in life and the responses I decide to make to those challenges. As a result of reading WAR AND PEACE, I believe we can all learn from adversity and become better people by participating fully in, and learning from, the obstacles we encounter in life. A passage from WAR AND PEACE that really brought this home for me was this one, which I found just now as I was leafing through the book:

"'They say: sufferings are misfortunes,' said Pierre. 'But if at once this minute, I was asked, would I remain what I was before I was taken prisoner, or go through it all again, I should say, for God's sake let me rather be a prisoner and eat horseflesh again. We imagine that as soon as we are torn out of our habitual path all is over, but it is only the beginning of something new and good. As long as there is life, there is happiness. There is a great deal, a great deal before us.'"

—Leo Tolstoy, War and Peace[4]

Example #3: Learning from the Lives of Others

Juan took my advice about writing quickly and writing about the very first person or event that came to mind in connection with a major life lesson. His first journal entry was quite powerful. It read as follows:

My grandfather Hernan, on the day I was to graduate from high school, took me out for breakfast. He said he knew I would be making my own decisions now that I was on the point of becoming a man. He told me he loved me very much and he was proud of me. He told me that it was fine to have a drink or even a few drinks now and then, but he also told me something I didn't know, that he had had a heroin addiction when he was a much younger man. He said there were times when he had nearly died, and there were other times when he wished he had died, while he was going through withdrawal. He asked me to promise him that I would never put a needle in my arm. I was so surprised by him telling me what he had told me about him having been an addict, and so moved by that, that I started to cry. I could tell that he wanted me to avoid a lot of pain that he had gone through personally, that he wanted to help keep me from hurting myself and others. I promised him I would never put a needle in my arm. There were a number of big lessons I learned from that talk. The first was that recreational drugs are not worth it, that they carry too heavy a price. And the second was that if you love someone you should try to find the right moment to share what you have learned in life with them. If you have the opportunity to make a difference in someone's life through your experience, you should do that. I also realized that he knew our time on this earth is short, and that the time to express love to someone is now, while you still can.

Example #4: *Love People Because They're People*

This next example comes from my life. Growing up, I was lucky to have parents and others in my life who taught me to treat people with respect and consideration. I was told countless times by the people I loved most, "Love your neighbor as yourself." And: "Treat people the way you would want to be treated." And: "Don't discriminate against people based on their race or religion or anything else." There were innumerable variations on this message.

But you know what? Even though I was taught these important lessons growing up, even though I knew intellectually that they were a vitally important part of family and social life, I had not internalized those lessons. I thought I had incorporated those lessons into my life, and I thought I was doing a pretty good job of living according to them. I did not realize it, but it turned out that I could do a much better job. There came a day when I had to acknowledge to myself that I had not yet completely built what my parents had taught me into my belief system. Before this day, what I had been taught by my parents was not part of me at the deepest level. After this day, I felt what they had taught me in my bones.

Let me tell you about what happened that day. About five years ago, I was in an airport in a city I cannot recall, heading home from a speaking engagement with my assistant, Sharon Miner.

Sharon and I had been working together for about three years by that point. We were great working partners; she and I had become a team, a well-oiled machine that served as the engine of my business. Sharon did not just support the logistical aspects of what I did; she challenged me, brainstormed with me, helped me create content, and helped me overcome major challenges. I called her my Director of Accountability; she was the heart and soul of my speaking business.

That day, we were headed home—me to St. Louis, Missouri, and Sharon to Amarillo, Texas. We arrived at the airport early. I noticed there was an earlier flight to Amarillo than the one Sharon was booked on. I told her, "Look, there's an earlier flight. You should get on it. You'll get home quicker." Sharon agreed. She wanted to get home early if she could. So we went up to the gate agent.

This is the part of the story where I need to tell you that Sharon is African-American. She said to the little bald man behind the counter, "Hello, I'm on this other flight. I want to get an earlier flight. Is there any room? Is there any chance I can go standby?"

And the airline worker looked her up and down, made a strange and dismissive expression with his face, and said in a derogatory tone, "I'm sorry, but you would *have* to have status to go standby on an earlier flight."

Not "*Do you* have such-and-such status with our airline?" Just: "You would *have* to have status to go standby on an earlier flight." Because she was a woman of color, he made the automatic assumption that Sharon did not and could not have the status necessary to go standby!

As it happened, Sharon had *platinum status* on that airline! She flew all the time! She was qualified to go standby at no charge. Not only that—she was qualified to go to the top of the list. But the little man behind the counter had not seen fit to ask about any of that.

Now, I was standing right by Sharon's side, and I heard every word of this exchange. When the man said that, the experience literally pushed me backwards physically. That is how stunned I was. I had to take half a step backwards. My eyes started to tear up a little bit.

At that moment, I felt for the first time what it was really like to be a person of color in the United States of America. To be instantly marginalized. Discounted. Dismissed. Based on absolutely zero meaningful information.

That man had looked at her and seen the color of her skin and made an assumption about who Sharon was as a person. And in that moment I felt one of the most horrific feelings I have ever experienced. I felt shame for the little bald man at the counter, shame for my country, and shame for myself at having made similar assumptions about people in the past.

I stepped forward, and I intervened. I said, "She's platinum with your airline. She qualifies." It just jumped out of my mouth.

The little man bristled but then realized he had made a huge mistake—and set about fixing it. He took care of the booking. I do not remember what was said after that point. It could not have been more than a few curt words on anyone's part. Once we got the booking straightened out, Sharon and I turned and walked off. I looked at Sharon as we were walking. I was still very close to tears.

I said, "I know you have talked about this a million times. But I have never physically experienced that kind of discrimination before. And this time I did. This time I got a glimmer of what it must be like to have to go through something like that on a regular basis."

That, for me, was a defining moment. That was a moment of understanding what it really meant to love another human being as myself. I deeply felt what Sharon was going through; I knew what was behind it from the airline worker's standpoint, too, because I realized that like him, I had made plenty of assumptions about people based on zero meaningful information. But I also knew that that could not happen again, because making those kinds of assumptions was the exact opposite of what I had taught people for years and what I had always said I believed.

That experience at the airport galvanized something deep inside of me. It was a defining moment—the moment when I realized in my gut that I could never participate in or support a situation like that ever again, even accidentally. I could never look at someone and prejudge them or make a determination about who they are or what they are capable of based on something superficial like the color of their skin. It may be easy to do that, but I realized in that moment that I could simply never allow myself to do it again. And I could never allow someone in my presence to do the same thing without my speaking up, regardless of whom I might offend.

That day in the airport, I realized what love your neighbor as yourself really means for me. It means, *Hey, love people!* It doesn't matter who the people are. It doesn't matter what they look like. It doesn't matter what they believe. It doesn't matter where they're from. Just love them. That's all that matters.

Up to the moment I had that experience with Sharon, the concept of "love your neighbor as yourself" existed mostly as an abstraction for me. After that experience, it became a practical reality in my life. It became something I knew I had to live by. I am now willing to tell anyone and everyone that I believe in that. I do not care what they think. It is part of who I am.

After that incident at the airport, I had the opportunity to think very deeply about the principle of "love your neighbor as yourself."

And I found myself going back to the verse in the Torah from which it sprang:

> "Do not seek revenge or bear a grudge against anyone among your people, but love your neighbor as yourself. I am the LORD."

Now, this is ancient wisdom, and for years I had it filed in that category: something important from my culture and my religion, something that was very old and very wise, something that I needed to pay attention to whenever I had the opportunity—a guideline I should aspire to when there was enough time and energy left at the end of my busy day. There was an intellectual fascination with this verse, because I considered it to be the starting point of a lot of interesting social and philosophical discussions down the centuries: To whom does the phrase "anyone among your people" refer? Who is my neighbor? Who *could* be my neighbor? And exactly how should one love one's neighbor as oneself? After that experience with Sharon at the airport, I realized that that verse had to be a central element of my code for living. It had to be something I took action on regularly. It had to be part of my belief system.

Now It's Your Turn

Using the examples you have just read, open your *Pivot!* Journal and write down three Source Experiences from your own life. Remember, each lesson should be personally important to you, something you are willing to live by right now. Each lesson should respect the rights of others, and each lesson should be different.

Go!

> "Truth is not a mathematical concept that needs to be proved with equations. Its singleness demands an intact moral compass, with certainties about what is good and bad." —Ece Temelkuran

Exercise #2: Notice the Common Threads

If you have completed the first exercise as I have laid it out, you now have three important life lessons to consider, each recorded in depth in your *Pivot!* Journal. What I want you to do now is step back and take a look at all three and notice what kinds of connections you see. Where did the big lessons come from? What do they have in common? Specifically, are there common elements in terms of *whom* or *what* you learned the lessons from, *when* you learned the lessons, or *how* you learned the lessons?

For instance, in Bill's case, he found, to his surprise, that two of the three major life lessons he had written about derived directly from the New Testament. You have already seen the one I shared with you about the Golden Rule, which had deep meaning for Bill; as it turned out, there was another passage from one of the Gospels (Matthew 5:14–15) about sharing one's light with the world that registered powerfully with him because of a musical production he had performed in when he was in college, *Godspell,* which used that passage as the inspiration for one of the numbers in which he performed. So in examining his three life lessons, Bill noticed that two of them came from the same source: the Christian Bible. Not what he expected, but an important connection nonetheless. In Bill's case, *whom* he learned the lessons from mattered a great deal.

Or consider what Jennifer discovered. She started out thinking that her Source Experience had connected to a particular college course… but after some consideration and self-examination, she realized that it was something very different that had led her to reassess the hardships and obstacles she had experienced in her own life. The critical event, she decided, had really come as a result of the instructor's decision to include *War and Peace* on the class syllabus. That was the *when*; revisiting the time frame helped her understand what had led to the reassessment. She had devoured the book. Reading *War and Peace* had connected her with a different—and for her, transformative—way of looking at the world: with compassion, with a desire to be of use to others, and with a deep sense of certainty that her journey in life could be meaningful to herself and the people in her circle. Tolstoy's view of the world, she realized, was all about contribution. And that, she discovered, was how she wanted to live.

In Juan's case, he closely examined the three life lessons he had uncovered—and determined that the experiences that drove them had all taken place in the year before his grandfather died. This was an intriguing piece of information, because it reinforced a clear pattern that had shown up in his journal writing: the three lessons all connected to discussions Juan had had with his grandfather during moments when the two of them had been alone together. Even after Juan's grandfather died, Juan still had remarkable moments of feeling his grandfather's presence in his life. "Sometimes it's like he and I are still spending time together, and he's just about to ask me if I want to play cribbage, which is something we did a lot, especially during the last few months we had with each other." The act of writing down life lessons reminded Juan that the year before his grandfather passed had been an especially important time in his life, a period when he had grown and matured a great deal due to his grandfather's influence. In Juan's case, *when* the lessons came along in his life made a big difference.

Finally, consider my example. I had been exposed to that verse from the Torah for virtually all of my life, but I think the teaching behind those words became part of my active belief system—something I had to consider non-negotiable in terms of the decisions I made and the everyday life I lived—only when I experienced it firsthand as giving me more insight on a *choice* that I could make differently. That direct experience of the massive impact connected to the personal choice to prejudge people based on their race, their religion, their gender, or any other factor changed me. It turned the abstract idea of "love your neighbor as yourself" into the enduring life lesson "I must not prejudge other people or allow prejudging to happen in my circle." Two other important life lessons on my list—that what I allow in my circle I condone, and that life is an adventure that I live actively when I live with integrity, respect, and significance—had similar origins. They both connected to personal experiences I have had about the direct and indirect impact of personal *choices* I could make—choices that had the potential to affect me and others to whom I was connected.

What I want you to do right now is to take as much time as you need to identify the common threads that connect the life lessons you have recorded in your *Pivot!* Journal. Specifically, I want you to answer these questions in writing:

Do these life lessons share any common elements in terms of *who* or *what* brought them to your attention? There may not be, but check to find out for yourself. Is there a common *text* from which the lessons emerged—such as the Torah, the New Testament, the novels of Tolstoy, or any other text to which you feel connected? Is there a common *person* who directly or indirectly shared these lessons with you or inspired you to learn them and put them into practice? When you think of these life lessons and your own ability to follow them, do you ever think in terms of what a specific individual in your life would have done if they had been facing the situation you face?

Do these life lessons share any common elements in terms of *when* you learned them and started following them? Is there any particular period of your life from which the lessons you wrote down emerged? Was there one breakthrough moment or breakthrough experience that connects two or perhaps all three of these lessons? Was there a period of important learning or growth relating to any of your life lessons that connected, for example, to the loss of a loved one? What other life lessons might present themselves now that you have identified some commonalities?

Do these life lessons share any similarities in terms of *how* or *why* they became important to you? Did they happen to unfold in similar ways, e.g., when you were faced with a given set of circumstances or had a particular kind of action to take or role to play? For instance, did they present themselves to you while you were teaching others or while you were being taught by someone? Do the lessons share any common themes or foundational concepts? If so, *why* do you think those common ideas presented themselves to you when you took on the task of writing down these lessons? What do the life lessons you identified suggest are most important to you as a person?

By this point, you should have at least three important life lessons you can examine closely and perhaps even discuss with others. It is likely you have identified a few more as you completed exercise 2. Write everything down.

Exercise 3: Find Your Source

The idea here is to identify the person, traditions, texts, or experiences that have had a strong, enduring positive influence on you, based on the life lessons and the commonalities you have uncovered in exercises 1 and 2. This is your Source. It may connect to one event in your life or to several. It is the point from which your good decisions and your growth as a person issue. You will know it when you find it.

Bill decided, after a long period of thought and reflection, that his Source was the words of Jesus that appear in the Gospels.

Jennifer came to the conclusion, as a result of completing this exercise, that her Source was the writings of Tolstoy, which she found to be imbued with a wisdom that transcended the world of fiction.

By the time Juan took on this exercise, he already had a very clear sense of who his Source was: his grandfather as he came to know him during their final year together.

For me, the Source of my good decisions and my growth as a person is the Torah. What happened to me during that remarkable experience with Sharon at the airport awakened me to the importance of the Torah in my life, and it inspired me to keep waking up to that importance as often as I lose sight of it, which is pretty regularly. The important thing is that I recognize it now as my Source. I trust it, and I consistently turn to it when I have any decision to make.

Each of us must find our Source on our own. This is a uniquely personal journey. This third exercise is worth taking some time on, and I strongly encourage you to complete it before you move forward in this book. It is vitally, even life-savingly important that you take the time to identify your Source. No one else can do that for you.

We must never judge other people on what their Source is, or try to convince them to use our Source. As long as a person's Source respects the rights of others, it is appropriate and it is right for that person.

> We must never judge other people on what their Source is, or try to convince them to use our Source. As long as a person's Source respects the rights of others, it is appropriate and it is right for that person. This is a personal journey for each of us.

When you do not know what your Source is, you are likely to feel confused and uncertain when the time comes for you to make a decision about something important—and you are all but certain to feel uncomfortable when you are facing a decision that has the potential to take you outside of your comfort zone. Without your Source, you are all on your own. You are improvising your way through life, based on superficial influences like short-term goals, passing emotions, very recent experiences, and the personalities and agendas of other people. You are also more likely to listen to the loudest voice in the room, which most of the time is not the right voice. Without your Source, you are far less likely to make decisions that serve you and others and far more likely to make poor decisions in challenging situations.

On the other hand, when you *do* know what your Source is, you have instant access to the foundation of your belief system. As a result, you find it relatively easy to make decisions, even the most important and potentially challenging ones, because you understand at a deep level what your Source would have you do—and, by extension, what you value most. You are able to eliminate the distractions.

Beliefs, Values, and Your Source Question

Beliefs and values overlap: they must be consistent with each other, and they must be supported by the actions you take and the decisions you make in life. If you *say* you value honesty and *say* you believe in telling people the truth, but your actions and your decisions go in the opposite direction, then you do not value honesty—and you must find a way to regain the value of honesty if it is truly part of your belief system!

One of the very best ways to gain clarity about your core values *and* your core beliefs is to consult your Source. A simple, powerful way to do this is to ask yourself a special kind of question that I call a Source Question. A Source Question sounds like this:

What would (my Source) do in this situation?

Or:

What would I do in this situation if I were fully aligned with (my Source)?

So, for instance, having completed this exercise, Bill might ask:

What would Jesus do?

Jennifer might ask:

What would I do if I were looking at this situation in the way Tolstoy would look at it?

Juan might ask:

What would Grandpa do?

And I might ask:

What would I do in this situation if I were aligned with the teachings of the Torah?

Take the time now right now to identify your Source in your *Pivot! Journal.* Do not be surprised if this takes a while. Invest the time. Once you know with certainty what or who your Source is, create your own Source Question using the examples above as a model.

Before we move on to the next exercise, let me suggest that you spend some time using your Source Question to get a clear fix on your own values. This Source Question reminds you that your values are your beliefs in action. Values are the active expressions of the very same idea that drives a core belief.

Beliefs are inward-facing and talk about how you view yourself and the world; they may or may not be something you share with others. Values are outward-facing and talk about that which is so important to you that if you happened to lose it, you would move heaven and earth to get it back. Values generally *are* shared with the outside world. You and I may believe very different things, but what we can connect and agree on are our values.

It is shared values that hold families, groups, and organizations together and unite them in a common Purpose. It is shared values that have the potential to unite the community, the nation, and the world in which we live when there is a crisis or an obstacle that affects us all. What makes a diverse team, a diverse family, a diverse society possible? What allows these gatherings of people to thrive, survive, and overcome challenges? Two things: the choice to respect the uniqueness of each individual's beliefs—and the choice to build bridges based on shared values.

> The choice to respect the uniqueness of each individual's beliefs and build bridges based on shared values is what makes diverse teams, families, and communities strong.

You can confirm for yourself that you have identified a value you are willing and eager to share with the world by checking to make sure that it is the active, outward-facing expression of a core belief that aligns with your Source. Thus, in my case, *I believe in "love your neighbor as yourself"* takes active form in the value RESPECT, since that is what you show someone when you love them as yourself. *I believe we are here to serve others* takes active form in the value SIGNIFICANCE, because helping other people attain significance in their lives is one of the highest forms of service. And *I believe in doing what's right* takes active form in the value INTEGRITY, since that is how doing the right thing is expressed in the real world.[5]

VALUES ARE BELIEFS IN ACTION.

BELIEFS ARE INWARD-FACING.

VALUES ARE OUTWARD-FACING.

Exercise 4: Begin Declaring Your Personal Code

Building on what you have accomplished in exercises 1–3, make a personal declaration of at least three core beliefs for which you are willing to take a stand, even if doing so is uncomfortable, unpopular, stressful, or temporarily painful. Make sure they originate from your Source. Make sure they respect the rights of others. Make sure they are each the answer to the question "What do you believe deep down inside?"

Taken together, these core beliefs constitute the beginnings of your Personal Code. In your *Pivot!* Journal, write down your core beliefs in a form you feel comfortable with, and then speak them aloud to someone close to you.

By way of example, here are Bill's core beliefs:

- No matter how dark it gets, there is always good in the world.
- Family comes first.
- I can do all things through God, who strengthens me.

And for the record, my core beliefs are as follows:

- *I believe in "love your neighbor as yourself."* This means not only that I strive to love others, even when it is difficult—but also that I strive to love myself, even when it is difficult. (This ties to my value of Respect.)
- *I believe we are here to serve.* Muhammad Ali is credited with saying the following: "The service you do for others is the rent you pay for your room here on earth." That captures the essence of this core belief perfectly. (This ties to my value of Significance.)

- *I believe in doing what's right.* If I know in my heart that a given course of action is the right thing to do, I believe that I am obligated to do the right thing, whether or not doing it happens to be convenient or popular. And if someone I trust sees me getting ready to do something we both know is wrong, I want to hear about it. (This ties to my value Integrity.)

Close-Up on the First Big Question

There are still a few important things to discuss about core beliefs before we move on.

First and foremost, recall that our core beliefs are the answer to the First Big Question: *What do I believe?* Notice that we *begin* with the core beliefs. That is not an accident. Our core beliefs are intimately connected to our Source. They shape our understanding of the world, and our understanding of the world, in turn, has a huge impact on our ability and willingness to Pivot when faced with a challenge.

Second, know that the most powerful core beliefs are those that are *consciously* taken on and *consciously* considered. This, for most of us, is the only path toward a truly *empowering* belief system. Many people do not really know what they believe at a very deep level. As a result, they cannot express or engage with constructive beliefs in a way that helps them to reset and claim full control of their own lives when they experience stress or challenges. People may be able to tell you exactly what they believe about themselves and the world—but their beliefs may be DISEMPOWERING. Their tragedy is that they have conditioned themselves over a long period of time to take on and reinforce disempowering beliefs that do not serve themselves or others. If you have ever met someone who was in the habit of blaming their misfortunes on the actions and choices of other people, rather than taking action and making choices based on the principle of being personally accountable for their lives, then you have encountered the kind of disempowering belief system I am talking about.

The effort you have made in this chapter is only the beginning. You need proof that what you have discovered about yourself and your beliefs actually works for you. Live these beliefs. Stress-test them. Return to them day after day, week after week, month after month. Do your core beliefs inspire you in moments of trial and challenge? Do you find it easy to stop what you are doing and consider whether what you are doing is in alignment with your beliefs? Do you make decisions more easily once you have engaged with your core beliefs, and do you find it easier to stick with those decisions? Do you feel better about yourself and your life's direction when you have made a decision in accordance with your core beliefs? Do you actually follow your core beliefs in your daily decisions, and do you find that periods of indecisiveness and inconsistency in your decision-making are few and far between? If this is what you are experiencing, then you are on the right track.

Your belief system is your compass in life. Having no compass is unacceptable. Having a broken compass is unacceptable. Keep at this until you get a compass that works.

If your belief system is not working for you, change it. If it is working for you, stick with it!

By taking conscious control of your belief system, by identifying your Source, and by clarifying and reinforcing the most important positive beliefs that align with your Source, you are placing yourself among the select few who assume direct control of their own choices, their own experiences, and their own responses to the world. That is a good place to be. And it is where every successful Pivot begins.

> Take a few minutes to answer these questions briefly in your *Pivot!* Journal.

- What do you believe about yourself?
- What do you believe about people?
- What do you believe about the world around you?

Notes

1. John F. Kennedy, Commencement Address at American University, Washington, DC, June 10, 1963, http://www.jfklibrary.org/archives/other-resources/john-f-kennedy-speeches/american-university-19630610.

2. John F. Kennedy quoted in Martin J. Sherwin, "One Step from Nuclear War: The Cuban Missile Crisis at 50: In Search of Historical Perspective," *Prologue: The Journal of the National Archives* 44, no. 3 (2012): 15.

3. Morten T. Hansen, "How John F. Kennedy Changed Decision Making for Us All," November 22, 2013, *Harvard Business Review*, accessed June 9, 2020, http://hbr.org/2013/11/how-john-f-kennedy-changed-decision-making.

4. Leo Tolstoy, *War and Peace*, trans. Constance Garnett (New York: Modern Library, 2002), 1275.

5. Values fall into four basic categories: *Foundational* values are the basis or groundwork on which everything else stands. They identify the one thing on which you will never, ever compromise. Foundational values speak to your character. *Relational* values affect the way in which two or more people behave toward and deal with each other. *Professional* values affect the level of quality and excellence with which you approach any undertaking. Your professional values determine the level of quality and excellence you deliver, regardless of what you happen to be doing or whether you are being paid to do that. *Community* values affect how you feel about, participate in, and support your community. A great list of core values ticks all four of these boxes.

Chapter 4

The Belief Test

ACTING IN ACCORDANCE with our Source is the ultimate test that each of us faces every day. This is the Belief Test. Passing this test means that our decisions are rooted in beliefs that align with our Source. When our actions do not align with our words, it means we are failing the Belief Test. It means we do not believe what we say we believe; instead, we believe whatever is convenient or popular at the moment. It means we are not living up to our full potential as human beings.

It is when we do not stick with our Source that we get ourselves into trouble. That is how we make bad decisions, decisions that do not align with who we really are. When our beliefs guide us toward the decisions that support our best self, then we are on the right path. This is why it is so important to identify, reinforce, internalize, and strengthen our positive, constructive beliefs—the beliefs that come from our Source, respect the rights of others, and connect us constructively to other people. We will need these beliefs as guidance, especially during times of stress, trial, and controversy.

So, when times are tough, do we make hasty concessions in order to pursue short-term goals, like being comfortable or liked by others?

Are we acting in our own interests, or are we acting in accordance with the dictates of our best self? Sometimes these two things can be the same, but not always! Consider that our best self is always motivated by some aspect of *service toward others.*

> Are we acting only in our own interests...or are we acting in accordance with the dictates of our best self? Consider that our best self is always motivated by some aspect of *service toward others.*

The Next Step: Purpose and Mission

If you have completed all the activities I have shared with you thus far, I am guessing that by now you have a much clearer sense of *what you believe about yourself* and *what you believe about the world in which you live.* I hope you do, and I hope the kind of clarity you are experiencing right now is the result of taking the time and investing the effort necessary to connect to your Source...and identify the unique belief system that best supports you as an individual.

> "Before you call yourself a Christian, Buddhist, Muslim, Hindu or any other theology, learn to be human first."
> —Shannon L. Alder

My challenge to you now is to take this to the next level. Now it is time to ask a couple of questions that will take you even deeper.

What do you believe about your Purpose?
And what do you believe about your Mission?

Addressing these powerful questions is the best possible way to consolidate your belief system and put it to work in a practical way. Once you know what you believe about your Purpose in life and about the Mission that supports that Purpose, you will find it easier to make sure that your words, actions, and decisions align with the person you are truly meant to be. The people who move forward with authority in their lives are those who are absolutely certain about what they are out to accomplish and why they are out to accomplish it. You can be one of those people…if you are willing to take on a potentially uncomfortable question, a question that most people do their level best to avoid: *Where are you headed in your life—and why?*

This question is foundational to anyone who is serious about Pivoting in response to challenges they face. Your ability to respond constructively to any obstacle is defined by three points: where you were yesterday, where you are today, and where you want to end up tomorrow. How can you possibly chart the direction you want to go if you do not have a clear sense of why you are where you are, how you got there, and where you want to go next? You must have full clarity about the trajectory of your life's journey if your aim is to Pivot—and that means you need full certainty about both your Purpose and your Mission.

Identifying your Purpose and the Mission that supports it is the fulfillment of your belief system. As it stands, you have made the first half of the journey by identifying your core beliefs. Your task now is to identify a Purpose that is consistent with the beliefs you have already identified and a Mission that arises out of that Purpose. Knowing what you believe about your Source, your Purpose, and your Mission is the trifecta of a strong belief system. Your Purpose is built on your Source. Your Mission is your Purpose in action.

> Your Purpose is built on your Source. Your Mission is your Purpose in action.

I have noticed that people who struggle when it is time to Pivot typically lack clarity about what their Purpose and their Mission is. If, right now, you are wondering what these terms really mean or how they will be reflected in your life, strap yourself in…and get ready for a moment of transformation.

Your Purpose: The Big "Why"

We are responsible for things. We are accountable to people. In order to achieve our own potential, we must help other people be their very best...and we must accept their help in becoming our very best. Accountability is the fulfillment of this principle and the practical application of these wise words:

> "If I am not for myself, who will be for me? If I am only for myself, what am I? And if not now, when?" —**Rabbi Hillel**

Your Purpose is the great WHY of your life, the reason you are here, the *service* you render joyfully to other people. Your Purpose is rooted in the Beliefs that proceed from your Source. Something extraordinary happens when you are fully engaged with your Purpose—a powerful feeling not only of being connected in a deeper way to the human family, but also of being in unity with a higher power, a higher calling. There is a feeling of being in more complete alignment with something far larger than ourselves. I call this feeling being On Purpose.

Releasing yourself to your Purpose means living your life On Purpose moment by moment. It means consciously accepting your Purpose as the guiding force of your life. It also means releasing yourself from all excuses. An excuse is a story that you tell yourself to sell yourself and try to sell to others, such as "I am too old/young/inexperienced/whatever to take on such-and-such a goal." That is a classic personally limiting story. Such a story is a lie. And telling yourself a lie is morally wrong!

> An excuse is a story that you tell yourself to sell yourself and try to sell to others. Such a story is a lie. And telling yourself a lie is morally wrong!

You will know when you have released yourself to your Purpose and moved past your excuses because you will feel a deep sense of calm. You will no longer feel that you are being pulled in multiple directions. You will know your right direction in life, whether you are having a good day or a bad day, whether events are lining up the way you expected them to or not. Decisions will become much easier for you. You will know immediately if you are acting in the service of your Purpose.

Getting clear on what you believe, and identifying and acting on your Purpose, is something we all need to do *regardless* of whether we are facing, or expecting to face, a challenge. Our lives may be going along nicely, but without a Purpose and a clear understanding of what we believe, we will not have any sense of what we *could* be doing, achieving, or enjoying. This is not just something we should do when we run into a roadblock. It is something we should do *before* we run into a roadblock, something that can even keep us from encountering the roadblock in the first place.

It is vitally important that you identify your Purpose. To do that, answer questions 1–4 below in your *Pivot!* Journal.

Exercise 1: What is most important to you?

Your personal Declaration of Purpose must connect to something that truly matters to you as an individual. So take some time to consider the following questions: *What is more important to you than anything else?* What is it absolutely essential that you give? To whom is it essential that you give it?

Exercise 2: Whom do you serve with joy?

If you believe you have found your Purpose, but your Purpose does not connect to another person, keep looking! If you believe you have found your Purpose, but your Purpose does not bring you joy, keep looking!

Take a few minutes to identify, in your *Pivot!* Journal, one or more specific people you have served when you were feeling true joy.

Exercise 3: What would a single sentence that expresses your life's service sound like?

Look carefully at what you have written down so far in your *Pivot!* Journal, and take all the time you need to distill your most powerful responses into a single sentence. Expect to invest a little time as you refine your words in search of clarity and connection with the service that arises directly from your Source.

The most powerful Purpose is always the one that gets the core idea across in the fewest number of words!

> *My Purpose is to help people discover their potential and be the best they can possibly be.*

A good friend of mine, a writer, used this exercise to create the following Declaration of Purpose:

> *To express devotion to my Creator by loving people and supporting them.*

Exercise 4:
How have you released yourself to your purpose?

Give examples of specific times when you fully released yourself to your Purpose. How did you know? How did you feel when it happened?

Your Mission

Your Purpose and your Mission are two sides of the same coin. Your Mission is your Purpose in action.

> Your Purpose and your Mission are two sides of the same coin. Your Mission is your Purpose in action.

To identify your Mission, answer questions 5–8 below in your *Pivot!* Journal.

Exercise 5:
How do you apply your purpose right now?

What specific activities do you engage in that support your stated Purpose? Make a written list in your *Pivot!* Journal.

For me, for example, activities that support my Purpose would include:

- Writing about accountability
- Speaking about accountability
- Individual coaching about accountability
- Helping people and organizations be more accountable
- Online engagement and reinforcement of principles that promote accountability
- Organizational development about building an accountable culture

Exercise 6:
How could you apply your purpose in the future?

What specific activities *could you* engage in that would support your stated Purpose?

For me, the list includes:

- Working with and inspiring young entrepreneurs to promote accountability
- Coaching younger students on living an accountable life
- Building up an international online accountability community

Exercise 7:
What is your mission?

In your *Pivot!* Journal, write a single sentence that reflects the ACTION side of your Purpose, based on a close review of the common points that you see in your responses to exercises 5 and 6. What is the larger undertaking or calling they all point toward? This is your Mission! Write it down. Keep it simple. You can revise it later if you need to.

The concise statement of my Mission is:

> *My Mission is to build a more accountable world.*

Exercise 8:
What three activities that connect *directly* to your mission bring you the most joy when you think about them?

Review the lists you have written in exercises 5 and 6 and select the ones that make you feel the most joy the instant that you read them. Select three activities that support your Purpose. Then write a sentence or two about each that clarifies what that activity means to you in practical terms. Taken together with your Mission, this is your Mission Narrative.

Here, for reference, is what my Mission Narrative looks like:

Mission

My Mission is to build a more accountable world. I serve my Mission through three specific activities:

Teach

I am a teacher. I educate people on ways to improve and be their best. I share new insights and ways of looking at issues, challenges, and opportunities. I share different ways of believing and thinking.

Inspire

Through the use of events, experiences, and evidence, I support the beliefs that I teach. This breathes life into the beliefs and helps people take action. I help people awaken to their true Purpose in life.

Support

I come alongside and help people take the "first step" in their new adventure. I provide ongoing encouragement, tools, and resources to help people stay on course. Change is difficult. We all face challenges throughout our journey. I stay ready to help others overcome those challenges and achieve the goals to which they aspire.

Notice that my Mission Narrative makes clear that my aim of creating an accountable world connects to three specific activities: teaching, inspiring, and supporting. It then briefly explains what each of those words means to me. After all, what I mean by "support" may not be the same as what you mean by it.

Here is the Mission Narrative that my friend the writer put together. Notice that it is his Purpose, expressed in specific *actions* that bring him joy.

Mission

As I Inspire, Connect, and Serve, God is with me on my Mission. God is helping me. God is guiding me.

Inspire

I harness the awesome power of the written word, and of story, to create narratives that move and engage fellow members of the human family. I help others express their big ideas in compelling written form. I inspire people to learn, feel, grow, and fulfill their true potential.

Connect

I connect with full presence to the people I love and the people I am learning to love. I support relationships with empathy, patience, and generosity.

Serve

I serve my Creator, and those whom He guides me to serve, with full devotion. I bear in mind as I do so that my time on earth is precious and limited.

I can do all things through Him who strengthens me.

At any and every moment, we face a fateful choice: being Off Purpose or On Purpose. We face a choice that defines us as people: the choice to neglect our Mission or pursue it with joy. When we choose to live On Purpose, when we choose to take actions that support our Mission and align with our beliefs, we have brought our belief system to life...and we are ready for any and every challenge. *We can Pivot only when we are On Purpose!*

> We can Pivot only when we are On Purpose!

Our Beliefs Are Always Illustrated by Our Actions

It is all too easy to make the mistake of imagining that building and implementing a positive belief system is just a matter of writing down or memorizing a few words. We get the right words down in black and white, and then we recite those words to ourselves or to others at moments of leisure. We proclaim: "This is what I believe."

That is not belief. That is public relations. Your beliefs are always and only reflected in your actions and decisions. *Belief is as belief does.* What you say you believe is meaningless—and yes, even counterproductive—if it is not backed up by action on your part.

> Your beliefs are always and only reflected in your actions and decisions. Belief is as belief does.

Right now, at this moment, you are acting out your belief system. Your actions and decisions are either bringing you closer to your Source...or pushing you further and further away from it. At any given moment, your actions and decisions are letting you know—and broadcasting to the world—exactly what you truly believe. It is your job to bring your decisions and actions into alignment with the words that you have chosen carefully to serve as compass points…the words that describe core beliefs that automatically take you back to your Source. Notice, though, that the words themselves are not beliefs— *until* you back them up with action!

This all may seem a little airy and abstract. Let me give you an example that will show you clearly that the distinction I am making is something you can implement immediately in your life in order to tap into your Source.

My former assistant, Sharon, had a fascinating way of testing whether I believed in something and was willing to back it up with action. She would ask me a question, and I would give her my answer and tell her what I wanted us to do and why I thought it was important to do it. She would look me in the eye and ask, "Is that what you really believe?"

I'd say, "Well, Sharon, I just told you that. Obviously it's what I believe, or I wouldn't have said it."

And she would keep this up for three, four, five, sometimes ten minutes. "Is that what you really believe?" Over and over again.

Eventually, I picked up on what she was actually doing. She was not repeating the question because she wanted to get on my nerves. She was repeating the question because she had not yet seen any signs of concrete *action* from me in support of what I said I believed…and she wanted to find out whether I was willing to *take* action and back up what I claimed to believe!

When she first started doing this, it just about drove me nuts. I wanted her to stop. But once I figured out the intention behind her question, I started asking myself some questions:

- Is this what I really believe?
- What action have I taken in support of this belief?
- What action am I willing to take in support of this belief right now?

Here is another example. Let's say that you have followed all the steps that have been laid out for you in this chapter, and you have determined that one of your core beliefs is the following:

- I believe in the fundamental equality of human beings AS human beings, and I believe that all human beings are entitled to respect.

You did not just pull this belief out of thin air. You invested the time, effort, and energy to create deep personal certainty about your Source—and you reached the conclusion that this core belief about the fundamental equality of human beings AS human beings proceeded directly from that Source. You wrote it down. You were inspired by it. You knew it identified the direction *you* are meant to go in *your* life and the person *you* are supposed to be.[1]

Then you were put to the Belief Test.

It did not feel like a test at the time. It felt like a chance to relax. Your boss invited you and your spouse out to dinner. He wanted to reward you for doing a great job, and he insisted on taking you and your loved one out to the fanciest restaurant in town—his treat. You and your partner happily accepted the invitation.

So there you are—you, your spouse, your boss, and his wife. You have each been enjoying a great meal. You have each had a little wine. The waiter comes and clears the dishes from the main course and asks if you would like to see a dessert menu. Your boss says "yes." Then, right after the waiter leaves, your boss makes a nasty racial joke at the waiter's expense. The boss's wife laughs loudly.

What do you do?

> **SCENARIO ONE:** You say nothing. You do not think the joke is particularly funny. In fact, you are personally offended by it. But you do not feel like offending your boss, so you quickly change the subject.

> **SCENARIO TWO:** You say to your boss, "Listen, I know that was meant to be funny, but I have to tell you, those kinds of jokes really do not work for me. Would you mind if we avoided that kind of humor when we are together?"

In Scenario One, you might imagine that you are upholding your belief system, because you did not laugh at the joke and you quickly made an effort to change the subject. But in reality, you betrayed your core beliefs and you stepped away from your Source, because you allowed the joke to pass unchallenged in your space. *When you believe something at the very core of your being, you consistently take action on it, even when doing so is inconvenient or uncomfortable.*

> When you believe something at the very core of your being, you consistently take action on it, even when doing so is inconvenient or uncomfortable.

Is Scenario Two easy? Maybe not. The first time you draw a line in the sand and defend it, you are likely to feel a little uneasy about what you are doing. But you know *why* you are doing it, and you find that it gets easier as you go along. Making decisions and taking action in accordance with your values defines you as a person of character.

> "Good timber does not grow with ease. The stronger the wind, the stronger the trees." —Thomas S. Monson

That which you allow in your space, you condone. When your beliefs are violated, you step up and do something about it if you are a person of character. That does not mean you quit your job, or insult your boss, or insist that he take back what he said, or make the exchange confrontational in any way. But it does mean you tell the truth and take a stand for what you believe deep down in your soul. It does mean you accept the consequences of taking action when failing to take action would be a violation of your core beliefs. Remember: you are following the foundational principle that to be defendable, your Source and your belief system must value people and respect the rights of others. It is worth making the effort to defend that. And most people will respect you for doing so.

> Never forget: To be defendable, your Source, your Purpose, your Mission, and your belief system must all value people and respect the rights of others.

Imagine a world in which people operate under the principle that what they allow in their space, they condone. Imagine a world in which everyone acts on, and defends, beliefs that value people and respect the rights of others. That is the world I want to live in. And that world starts with you and me.

> That which you allow in your space, you condone.

Your Personal Code

This book is about the development of a personal code. Note, though, that your personal code is much more than your beliefs. It is the combination of your beliefs, your focus, and your commitments. In the next chapter, we will take a deep dive into that second element: your focus. Before you do that, though, please take on the following questions.

> You have done a lot of work up to this point to gain clarity on what you really believe. Before you move forward, take just a few minutes now to answer these questions briefly in your *Pivot!* Journal—one sentence maximum for each response!

- What do you believe about your Source?
- What do you believe about your Purpose?
- What do you believe about your Mission?

Note

1. Note, though, that the fact that you believe something does not qualify you to start acting as a duly authorized member of the Belief Police. It is not your job to change anyone's beliefs but rather to live your own.

Chapter 5

The Frankl Factor

VIKTOR FRANKL was an extraordinarily gifted author, neurologist, and psychiatrist—who also happened to be a Holocaust survivor. He spent time as a prisoner in Theresienstadt, Auschwitz, Kaufering, and Türkheim.

From where I sit, Frankl is one of the great thinkers of the twentieth century, in part because of his authorship of the remarkable book *Man's Search for Meaning* and in part because of his development of what is known as the logotherapy method, now acknowledged as a major school of psychotherapy. Both the book and the school of therapy are built on the same foundation: Frankl's "Will to Meaning" principle. This principle holds that the primary motivational force of any human being is to find meaning in life. Just as important for Frankl was the idea that each of us has the power—and indeed, the duty—to find that meaning for ourselves, both in terms of our big-picture life goals and, crucially, in terms of what a given experience means to us. We get to determine meaning for ourselves. No one else can do it for us.

I will share with you my favorite quote from Frankl:

"The one thing you can't take away from me is how I choose to respond to what you do to me. The last of one's freedoms is to choose one's attitude in any given circumstance." —**Viktor Frankl**

If that observation from a survivor of Auschwitz does not inspire you to Pivot, I do not know what will.

Our second Big Question is What do I focus on? And in answering it, our challenge is to leverage what I have come to know as the Frankl Factor: our own ability to choose how we will respond to what is taking place, our attitude in any given circumstance, and the direction of our mental energy. Each of us has that power to choose. Do we focus on what we can control, as opposed to what we cannot control?

When we focus on what we cannot control, we make excuses and bring fear into our life; when we focus on what we can control, we make decisions and we get results. Harnessing the power of focus in any given moment is the same thing as choosing for ourselves what that moment really means. And that is a truly extraordinary power, a power that I believe has the potential to transform any and every human life.

When we focus on what we cannot control, we make excuses and bring fear into our life; when we focus on what we can control, we make decisions and we get results.

A Question of Attitude

We always—repeat: *always*—have a choice about how to respond to what is happening in our lives. The only thing that is up for debate is whether we will convince ourselves otherwise.

The fact that we may experience strong emotions in certain situations *does not* mean we lose the capacity to choose our attitude. This is simply a matter of noticing the difference between what we can and cannot control. *Once we recognize the difference between what we can and cannot control, we are connecting to the ability to choose our attitude.* There are some things that are not—and have never been—under our control. It is our job to notice what those things are. As for emotions: they are part of the human experience. We honor them. We do not have to be ruled by them. It has been said that emotions are like waves on the ocean: we cannot stop them from coming, but we can choose which ones we pull out our surfboard for and ride on.

Ultimately, focus is simply a question of attitude. It is a matter of getting into the habit of asking ourselves, *Is this something I can control or something I cannot control?*

The mere act of asking such a question is instantly calming. One of the things we can *always* control is what our conscious, chosen response to a given situation is going to be. If our attitude is one of blaming, judging, and playing victim, then that is one way of living. If our attitude is one of connection, compassion, and assuming that we are the ones whose decisions and actions have the most impact on the quality of our life and the lives of others, then that is a very different way of living. What we focus on *matters*. And unless we are aware of that and are acting on our awareness, we are not living up to our full potential as human beings. That is the reality we all face.

> What we focus on matters.

We can instantly maximize our potential. We can instantly transform our lives, no matter what challenge we face. We simply have to *choose* how we will respond.

The Second Big Question Is Different from the Others

This second question in the sequence of the Three Big Questions—*What do I focus on?*—is fundamentally different from the other questions you are learning about in this book. What makes it different? You have a whole lot of leeway when it comes to your beliefs and your commitments. You can build those up from scratch in any way you want. When it comes to focus, however, you have zero leeway. This part of the program is non-negotiable.

The major issue we face is: Are we focusing on something we cannot control or something we can control? Very often, when we try to control things, we find that we get bogged down. If we try to control *people*, we will find ourselves bogged down even more. We cannot really control people. We may try to manipulate them with money, or with blame games, or with praise, but none of those tactics really work. We need to recognize that.

- There are some things we definitely *can* control, like our internal dialogue, our attitude, and our decisions about what a given event means and the actions we take.
- There are some things we *cannot* control, like the economy, the weather, or what our competition is doing.
- Then there are things we can *try* to control but cannot, like people—what they think, what they feel, what they do, and how they act. (We may be able to influence people, but we certainly cannot control them.)
- There are things that are *out of control*, like your inventory, a teenage boy's bedroom, or a forest fire. What do you do with a situation that is out of control? You work to bring it back into control.

The point is, we need to understand which of those four categories we are looking at. Understanding the difference between the things that we can control and the things that we cannot control is usually where the most important conversation is going to be. When you try to control something that you cannot possibly control—how someone else feels about you, for instance—you are taking on an impossible task. The Second Big Question, *What am I focusing on?*, serves as an important reminder of this reality.

When you answer the Second Big Question authentically, honestly, and with full presence in the moment, you accept that the question applies to every single waking moment of your life. It is a plug-in. It is a piece of software that is running whether you want it to be running or not. You have the task of choosing what you focus on, whether you want that task or not. You and you alone can choose to be present in your own thought process. No one can do that for you, and leaving it undone is not an option if you expect to Pivot.

When you take on this Second Big Question, you are agreeing to notice not just *when* you are focusing on something you cannot control, but also *how* you can take action to change your focus back to something you *can* control. You are taking on the necessity of doing that shift back to what you can control at every possible opportunity.

The Morality of Focus

By consciously letting go of what you have no power over, you are choosing to focus on what you can have power over and influence. That is an empowering place to be. That choice, made over and over and over again, projects you forward. It is important to understand that this is a *moral* choice. It is morally *right* to focus on that which you can control and influence and morally *wrong* to focus on that which you cannot control and influence. Why do I say that? Because if you spend your precious time obsessing about what you cannot control, you inevitably make excuses and poor decisions—decisions that hurt yourself and others. Hurting others, when you have the option not to, is wrong.

The instant we choose to focus on things we cannot control, fear takes over and shuts us down. In a matter of seconds, we move from a mindset of possibility, abundance, and connection to a mindset of scarcity, lack, and worry that makes it impossible for us to give and serve. The only antidote to this syndrome is to *focus on that which we can control!*

Make no mistake: if we choose to take on this Second Big Question, we are making what we choose to focus on part of our moral code!

So for instance: If we blame the weather, the economy, or anything else that lies outside of our control for our attitude toward others, the choices we make in our relationships, or the success of our business, that is wrong. It is not just an ineffective or inaccurate decision. It is a violation of what we know to be right. It is an excuse, a story we are telling ourselves and trying to sell to others. It is just as wrong as cheating someone, hurting someone, or telling a lie about something important. It *is* a lie about something important!

Or: If we spend half an hour complaining about a work colleague to a third party, without taking our issues to the person who can do something about what we are raising, *that is morally wrong*. It is not just a waste of time. It is not just a waste of energy. It is an excuse and a story and a violation of our moral code. The only way to right the wrong is to go to the person we have the problem with and work it out with them one on one. Pretending we do not have the ability or the strength to talk about what is bothering us with someone who is doing something we have a problem with is an excuse. It is a story we tell ourselves and try to sell to someone else. And it is a conscious choice to step out of alignment with our Source.

Start noticing whether what you choose to focus on, and what you choose to say and do based on what you focus on, aligns with your Source. Start noticing when you are making an excuse rather than a decision.

You really can control how you think about people and situations. You really can control what you focus on and choose to take action on. You really can decide when it does not make sense to put the power of your focus on things that you cannot control. For instance: You cannot control how other people act. You can control only how *you* act.

Focus your attention in a positive way on that which you can have a positive impact on. Draw a big black line between those actions and relationships…and the actions and relationships that you *cannot* affect in a positive way. Make a decision right now to stay on the right side of that line.

If your moral code allows you to focus consistently and automatically on that which you cannot possibly have any control over or impact on, *your moral code is flawed and does not serve you*. It needs to be changed.

A moral code is either variable or it is fixed. If you choose to take on the Second Big Question, you are choosing to take on a moral code that is fixed, consistent, and not optional. You are choosing to take on a moral code that says you have a personal right and duty to control your own power of focus, not just sometimes, but all the time. You are choosing to invest the precious energy of your attention on situations and relationships that you can improve. Your job is to make your own focus *conscious* and *positive*. Period. Is that easy? Maybe not. But who said it was always going to be easy to do the right thing?

Consider the person who habitually focuses on whatever bobs to the surface or makes the most noise, the person who regularly focuses on things they cannot control. This person tends to build anxiety and discomfort not only into their own lives, but into the lives of the people around them. That is not who we want to be!

Then consider the person who makes a habit of *choosing* what to focus on, the person who chooses over and over again to focus on that which is under their control. This person tends to be positive, focused, grounded, calm, and levelheaded…and tends to inspire and empower the people with whom they interact or connect to be the same way. This person helps the people around them to worry less, achieve more, and make better choices about what *they* will focus on. That is what knowing what one believes and knowing what one wants to focus on means: it means bringing a sense of calm to any and every situation in which you find yourself.

We All Have a Choice

No one I have ever met has exercised 100 percent total control over their mental focus at all times. Everyone I have ever met and considered a role model accepted, as a personal priority, the task of noticing when their focus had landed on someone or something they could not control and then shifting that focus onto a conscious *choice* about their own attitude and response.

When you take on this second question, not as a momentary diversion but as a foundation for ethical living, you take on the decision not to waste your time, your attention, or your emotional energy on things that are beyond your control. Your job is to *notice* habitual patterns of thought and action that don't support you. You may not be able to completely keep them from presenting themselves, but you *can* remind yourself that you have a choice about whether to indulge them. And you can start asking better questions.

P.S.: When you do notice yourself going off-track, be compassionate with yourself about that. Do not run a guilt trip on yourself. Move seamlessly and without blaming yourself into questions like, "What *do* I have control over? What *can* I do? How *can* I have a positive impact in this situation?"

Life is short. None of us is perfect. All we need to do is wise up, shift gears, and then move on—while bearing in mind that it is just as important to show compassion to ourselves as it is to show compassion to others.

> "Who will you love if not yourself? Other people? How can you love someone for anything but their raw, naked humanity? How can you say you love someone if it is not for their flaws and quirks, snorts and hurts, triggers and tears? Anything else is not love. It is idealization. And, as long as you do it to yourself, you will do it to everyone. You will not love anyone or anything until those eyes in the mirror soften up and embrace the beauty that is already within." —**Vironika Tugaleva**

Choice Points and Mindfulness

Each and every situation we encounter is a choice point and an opportunity to take on the Second Big Question through mindfulness.

Each and every situation we encounter is a choice point and an opportunity to take on the Second Big Question through mindfulness.

The Second Big Question is all about transforming your world, and transforming your world requires mindfulness. That is another way of saying that it requires you to be present in your own thought process. Mindfulness means cultivating self-awareness and noticing the choices you have made, why you made them, what the implications of those choices were, and what choices you can make now. Again, you are not beating yourself up over a poor choice you made. You are simply noticing what happened and learning from the experience. You are saying to yourself, "This is what happened, and this is how I am working on it." This is mindfulness in action.

Over time, you will come to notice the choice points as they are happening, so you can make decisions that match up with your Source the first time around, as opposed to stumbling around in the dark, as though you had no Source at all! The goal, over time, is to notice the choice points before you make a decision—so that you can make a decision that aligns with your Source and move forward in a way you can be proud of.

If a given course of action is not one you would be proud to share with your family over the dinner table, that is a flashing red light suggesting that you have been making excuses and have not been fully present in your own thought process.

If a given course of action is not one you would be proud to share with your family over the dinner table, that is a flashing red light suggesting that you have been making excuses and have not been fully present in your own thought process.

A Lesson from Baseball

Major league baseball players have a process they use to create awareness of a specific area or skill set with which they struggle. That process starts with giving the area where they struggle a special name. They call it *the hole.*

Every batter has a hole. A hole is a persistent weakness in a batter's hitting routine. A certain batter might be the league MVP, with 40 home runs to his credit and 125 runs batted in—but he still has a hole he must close. There is some pitch that ties him up, some pitch that opposing pitchers know they can use to increase the odds of getting him out and decrease the odds of him hurting them with his bat. Let's say the pitch this particular slugger hates is a high-and-outside fastball. The word gets around the league pretty fast: *This guy is dangerous, but you know what? If you can get him to chase the high-and-outside fastball, he always pops it up.*

Every batter in the big leagues (or any other league) has a hole, a pitch or area on which he needs to work. Let's say you are that big-leaguer. Every time you take batting practice, your main priority is going to be to *get better at hitting the high-and-outside fastball!* That is part of your conditioning routine as someone who seeks excellence. And excellence starts with noticing the pitch that gives you trouble. If you spend enough time in practice closing your hole, you can learn to make adjustments and improve your game. And since you are a big-league hitter, you are all about improving your game! Right?

What is true of major league hitters is just as true of us. If we want to make the very most of our own potential, if we want to get serious about focusing on that which we can change (as opposed to that which we cannot change), we will want to identify exactly what our own hole looks like when it comes to controlling our mental focus…and we will want to learn how to close that hole. We will want to learn to *notice* what "pitches" consistently give us trouble. And we will want to practice dealing with them creatively so that we can make the adjustments that will help us improve our game. And here is the biggest shift of all: we want to start being *grateful* for the times we see a "high-and-outside fastball" coming at us, because we know that each and every time we *notice* a situation that could cause us to respond unproductively, what we are really getting is an opportunity to practice strengthening one of our weak spots—so we can close our hole.

You must identify your own equivalent of the high-and-outside fastball. No one else can do that for you. You must figure out what you need to work on in terms of your own personal focus. Learn to recognize the pitch that gives you problems as it is bearing down on you. Be grateful for it. Remind yourself that it represents a chance for you to improve your conditioning and eventually to improve your execution.

So let's assume you are standing at the front desk of the hotel that you want to check into. It is late at night. You have been on three different flights, missed a connecting flight because of an airline's delay, and paid a significant amount of money for the privilege of booking the next available flight so that you could arrive in your destination city two and a half hours later than you were supposed to. You have an important commitment first thing tomorrow morning. And the clerk at the front desk is having some problems with his computer. He tells you he cannot find your reservation. Five minutes go by. Still no progress.

At this point, you may be tempted to think things like, "This front-desk person is totally unqualified for the job. Doesn't he realize that a lot of his customers have been traveling all day and have no time for him to learn how to find a reservation? Who on earth hired this guy?" And after just a few minutes of this kind of thinking, you may be tempted to say or do something that is totally inconsistent with one of your stated core beliefs: *I believe in supporting other people, empowering them, and doing everything I possibly can to help them to fulfill their true potential.*

Before you make that mistake, your job is to *notice that a high-and-outside fastball is headed your way.* This is the pitch you are working on! Take a deep breath. What is really happening here is that you have a conditioning moment to take advantage of. You have some *noticing* to do before you say or do anything.

The very first thing you want to notice, if you happen to find yourself in this situation, is that you do not know the whole story. You do not know what this person is up against. For instance, you do not know if he is distracted by some major personal challenge. If he is, that is not something you can control. Similarly, you cannot control whether the person at the front desk is qualified for the job or has been trained well. Likewise, you cannot control the decision of who gets hired to work at the hotel. By the same token, you cannot control hiring decisions that have already been made! So your initial internal dialogue about this person's perceived lack of qualifications is a total washout when it comes to making the best possible answer to the Second Big Question. *Notice* that in asking yourself questions like *Who on earth hired this guy?* your focus has shifted to things you cannot control. Take another deep breath. Center yourself. Then take your best swing at that high-and-outside fastball.

You go digging through your records and find your reservation and confirmation number on your phone and provide that to the clerk. Then you say, "I know computers can be a pain sometimes. I appreciate all you are doing." Those responses would be consistent with your belief system. Just be present with the situation. Do not judge it. Do not manipulate it. Experience it.

> "To think in terms of either pessimism or optimism over-simplifies the truth. The problem is to see reality as it is."
> —Thích Nhất Hạnh

Your decision-making and your actions can be totally consistent with your beliefs…*if* you make conscious choices about what you want to focus on. If you choose to focus on what you cannot control—for example, the skill level of the person at the desk, the economy, or the weather—you are popping that ball up into the glove of a waiting infielder or striking out. That is called beating yourself.

When you allow yourself to focus on that which you cannot control, you will inevitably find that you are making excuses and that those excuses become rationalizations for undermining your own most deeply held beliefs. It sounds like this: "*Normally* I support people and help them grow to make the best contribution they possibly can, but *this* time I was justified in not doing that because (fill in your favorite excuse here: "I had a hard day!" "I missed my flight!" "They hired an idiot!")."

This kind of thinking is a downward spiral. When we choose to perpetuate it, we are walking ourselves into a world where excuses carry the day. Excuses are the graveyard of our ability to Pivot.

> Excuses are the graveyard of our ability to Pivot.

The only way to avoid that graveyard is to start *noticing what is really happening.* Notice the high-and-outside fastball: "This is one of those situations in which I often slip up. I am tired, *and* I feel like the frontline service being delivered is not up to par. I need to get better at responding to this situation. I need to take a deep breath and think twice before I say or do anything here."

You can always control your *attitude* and your *response.* What *attitude* would your Source point you toward in this situation? What *response* would your Source have you make?

You cannot control where you have come from. You can always control where you are going.

> You cannot control where you have come from. You can always control where you are going.

Exercise #1: Spot the Hole, Part One

Write this in your *Pivot!* Journal:

BIG QUESTION NUMBER TWO: WHAT DO I FOCUS ON?

Consider that we all have situations that are likely to cause us to stop focusing on that which we can control...and start focusing on things we cannot control (for instance, being angry at other drivers when we are late getting to an appointment). Take a few minutes now to list at least FIVE situations where this is highly likely to happen to you. Record these in your *Pivot!* Journal.

Exercise #2: Spot the Hole, Part Two

Over the course of the next 24 hours, *notice* when you move into the headspace of excuse-making by fixating on that which you cannot control. Notice which of the five situations that you identified came into play. Identify any new situations that you might not have anticipated.

Each time you have a lapse in your focus, write down a brief sentence about it in your *Pivot!* Journal, identifying exactly what happened and how you created an excuse about it (for instance, "I blamed the traffic for my being late to the meeting, when in fact I was the one in charge of all my actions and decisions, and I could have left earlier and taken the traffic into account if I had wanted to."). Include the time when the event happened, and identify any people your excuse may have impacted.

Exercise #3:
Spot the Hole, Part Three

Closely review *all* of the entries you made over the course of that 24-hour period. Identify the *one* situation where you were *most* likely to start making excuses and start focusing on that which you do not control (for instance, when you choose not to give yourself enough time to arrive at your destination with 15 minutes to spare). Again: an excuse is a story we tell ourselves and sell ourselves and try to sell to others. Spot the story you are most likely to tell yourself during the course of any given day. This is your hole. Close it!

Please do not move on to the next chapter of this book until you have completed all three of this chapter's exercises and also answered the following questions.

- What is a story you are likely to tell yourself about why you cannot live your Purpose?
- What does your Source have to say about that story?
- In one sentence, what is your high-and-outside fastball?

Chapter 6

The Focus Test

AT ANY GIVEN MOMENT, you have total and absolute control over what you choose to focus on. Exercising that control not only has a powerful positive impact on you, but it also has a powerful positive impact on those who matter most to you.

For instance: If you are a leader who is looking for ways to motivate your team and inspire them to move forward in a positive way, and in particular if you are looking for ways to change people's behaviors, you will want to embrace the Second Big Question with both arms and hold on to it tightly. *Directing your own focus is always the first essential step to directing the team's focus.* This is a major test for leaders. (What follows about focus and leadership is meant primarily to be applicable to leaders in the workplace, but please note that it is broadly relevant to *all* relationships.)

All too often, leaders try to control people with a combination of financial incentives and blame. As we have seen, it does not work. Truly effective leaders understand that people are looking for more in life than a paycheck. Truly effective leaders do not have time to worry about who is to blame. They know the blame game is irrelevant. They might reach a point where they realize that they need to take a different approach in terms of their staffing decisions, and they might take that on as a personal choice that is part of something they control…but they will not waste time blaming other people or trying to make the people on their team feel bad about themselves. They know that is counterproductive.

Think back on the most effective leader you have worked with, the person who made you feel good about yourself and the tribe you had chosen to be part of. Think of the leadership style of the person at the head of that tribe. My guess is that the leader did not routinely play the blame game, did not call people names, and did not engage in playing the victim. My guess is that they had no time for doing any of that when they found themselves facing a challenge. They were too busy focusing on what they could do to bring about a positive resolution to whatever situation they faced. They did not want to waste a choice point! They knew that blaming others, calling them names, and engaging in high drama only made the job of addressing the challenge more difficult. Because they were taking on the Second Big Question (whether they called it that or not), they were less invested in perpetuating the problem and more invested in solving it.

Truly effective leaders know that blame does not solve problems. Accordingly, they do not blame others for *anything, ever*—including the situations where people with whom they work blame *them* for things. Truly effective leaders focus on what really matters—what they can do with the choice point that is sitting in front of them right now. They focus on what they can personally affect in a positive way, and they take that on fully and without hesitation or reservation. They focus on supporting the people around them. *This trait is what makes them leaders!*

If we are the leader and someone on our team dropped the ball, that reality is now part of history. It happened. It is like the Civil War or any other event from the history book. It is a closed event. We can study it. We can learn from it. We can make better decisions based on what we know happened. We can use what happened to shape our perspective on what is taking place right now. *But we cannot make it unhappen.* The fact that someone dropped the ball and made a mistake is no longer something we can control. What we can control is the quality of the questions we ask *after* someone has dropped the ball. As leaders, we can choose to move away from questions like "What on earth were you thinking?" Or "Didn't I tell you to watch out for so-and-so?" (Those kinds of questions focus our attention and our team member's attention on things in the past that cannot be controlled or even influenced now.) And we can move toward questions like "What can I do to help?" And "How can we fix this?"

What keeps that from happening? Why do so many people placed in leadership roles fail the primary test of leadership? Why do they ask questions like "Didn't I tell you about so-and-so?" Simple: They did not take on the Second Big Question.

One of the biggest reasons that team and company leaders do not take on the Second Big Question is that they get distracted by their own drama. They find ways to recruit others into their own little soap opera. Here is how it often plays out: Something bad has happened to them in their lives—there was some event or relationship that caused a problem that never got resolved. That problem has stayed unresolved for years or even decades. As a result, the person grew so used to locking themselves into that one difficult part of their lives and looking at themselves in a particular way that they convinced themselves they no longer had choice points at certain critical moments.

They sold themselves on the story that they "have to" respond toxically to certain situations—such as, to give one of the most common examples, situations where they perceive that someone is "letting them down." So, a situation where they feel let down by a team member comes up, and instead of responding to that moment pragmatically they find a way to replay that event or relationship from their past, usually without even realizing what is happening. They decide that they "have to" respond in a certain way. They lock themselves into their emotions from the past so automatically and with such intensity that they have no idea whom they are really talking to when they try to corner a subordinate with a question like "What were you thinking?" Very often, they are actually talking to a close family member, not a work colleague at all!

My experience is that when a person is replaying some endlessly recycled personal drama by posing such questions, they are almost always returning to some incomplete conversation with someone or something from their own past. Very often, these leaders take on a "woe is me" outlook on their relationship with the world at large—or, just as unproductively, a "woe is you if you let me down" outlook. *This kills teams.* For leaders stuck in this rut, the Second Big Question presents an opportunity for major personal and organizational growth—an opportunity to distinguish, in a healthy way, what is happening right now from what happened long ago. And once we make that critical distinction, we can focus on what we choose to make the experiences in our own lives, past and present, *mean.* This is perhaps the highest and most powerful application of the Second Big Question.

"Adversity introduces a man to himself." —H. L. Mencken

Let me give you a personal example of what I mean by all of this. My father-in-law, and one of my most important mentors, is named Mendel Rosenberg. He is in his nineties now, and he has been one of the most important people in my life for at least four decades. Mendel has been every bit as much of a father to me as my birth father was. Not only that, we were business partners.

There are a lot of things I could tell you about Mendel that relate to the vitally important question of how to direct your personal focus, but as we approach the question of how one's personal focus supports the ability to Pivot, I want to focus on his character.

A big part of Mendel's character is his habitual outlook on life, which was and is relentlessly positive. He is a master of looking on the bright side. He is the eternal optimist. The single greatest lesson I learned from Mendel was that I always had a choice when it came to deciding what something meant, and specifically that I could always choose to see the best in people rather than the worst in them. Mendel has, for as long as I have known him, had a remarkable talent for making people feel good about themselves. Even when there was a major problem to address, he has always looked for ways to redirect people and relationships toward the positive. He sees problems as opportunities to improve relationships.

I recall one instance where there was a plant manager who had been with our company for nearly two decades who had made some really terrible decisions, decisions that had had a major adverse effect on our business. Mendel found a way to ease this man into a different situation—and in fact made a financial investment that basically set him up in his own business as a supplier to our company. He did all of this rather than fire the man.

This was a textbook example of Pivoting in a leadership role. It turned out to be the best business decision for everyone. The point is, my father-in-law chose to focus on relationships and loyalty, which mean a great deal to him. They are how he expresses optimism. If he can find a way to see the best in someone, if he can identify a possibility for interacting together that honors an existing relationship and extends possibility in all directions, he will find a way to do that.

Mendel has used the power of focus to create meaning and Purpose in his life where it would have been easy to embrace cynicism, despair, and darkness. He is a master at posing the questions *What does this experience mean, and what do I choose to make it mean?* This is the essence of directing your focus. I got a great life lesson from Mendel: I always had the right, and the duty, to ask those two questions.

Mendel's unfailingly strong relationships with his family, with his employees, with his vendors—with *everyone*—were the practical expression of his Purpose. His major goal in life, I believe, was to make sure that his family, his company, and all of his relationships pointed people toward practical, sustainable expressions of the transcendent faith and optimism that had seen him through challenging situations in his own life, of which there were many. That was his service. He wanted to find as many ways as he possibly could to create connections and solutions that made that faith and optimism a reality in the lives of other people.

The next time you are inclined to take a "woe is me" approach to your life experience, ask yourself the questions Mendel taught me to ask: *What does this experience mean? What do I choose to make it mean?*

Take a few minutes to answer these questions briefly in your *Pivot!* Journal.

- What is the service you provide joyfully to others?
- Why do you choose to serve others in this way?
- What does serving other people mean to you?

Chapter 7

It's Personal

ALL EFFECTIVE LEADERSHIP, meaning both leadership in our own lives and the successful fulfillment of our role as a team or organizational leader, is rooted in accountability. And accountability is rooted in commitments—specifically, commitments to other people.

The commitments always begin with us and extend outward to others, which is what makes the Third Big Question—*What am I committed to?*—so powerful and so life-changing.

These interrelated concepts of commitment and accountability are commonly misunderstood. All too often, they are misunderstood by the very leaders who are best positioned to put them into practice and have a positive impact on their team, their organization, and the world at large.

> "The goal of many leaders is to get people to think more highly of the leader. The goal of great leaders is to get people to think more highly of themselves." —J. Carla Northcutt

I have worked with many leaders over the years, and one thing that I have learned to recognize quickly is a lack of clarity on the concept of commitment.

> Here is one of the most obvious signs that you may be missing the whole concept of commitment as a leader: you have a major decision to make that you know could have a negative impact on people, and you disengage from the emotional aspect of the decision and say something like this: "This is not personal—It's business."

I have news for you: it is personal. Every interaction that involves people is personal. If the decision you are about to make is going to have a potentially negative impact on people who count on you for leadership, *you need to feel that impact yourself ahead of time* before you confirm the decision. You need to experience it yourself, to the degree that you can, before you ask anyone else to experience it. Why? For the simple reason that you must have as full as possible a direct and personal understanding of how your decision is going to impact the people to whom you have made commitments.

If your decision-making process is not personal in this way, *you are not an accountable leader,* because you have overlooked or ignored personal commitments to the people who count on you. And not only that—if you are not even bothering to understand, on a personal level, whether the commitments you have made to people are being fulfilled, you have failed both as a leader and as a person.

Here is another sign that you may be missing the whole concept of commitment in leadership: you say things like, "I have 35 problems…and each of them has a first name." (Yes, I have heard plenty of leaders say something like this.)

The people who are looking to you for leadership are not problems. They are human beings. If you objectify them, minimize them, or otherwise convince yourself that they are a burden and a hindrance to you, then you have no right to call yourself a leader. The minute you stop thinking of the people who count on you *as* people, you have stepped away from the commitments they are counting on you to fulfill to them, for them, and on their behalf.

Here is another thing leaders who are unclear on the concept of commitment often say: "I am holding you accountable for X."

This is utterly unworkable. Even the phrase "I am holding you accountable" reflects a deeply flawed understanding of accountability. Accountability is all about *our* commitments to people, *our* approach to relationships, *our* willingness to be interdependent. Accountability is never about leadership trying to manipulate people in order to serve the leader's agenda.

> And here is one more sign that you as a leader might be missing something important when it comes to understanding the basic concept of commitment: you look a team member in the eye and say, "You've got to earn my trust."

That is 180 degrees backwards. If you are the leader, you have to earn *their* trust. If you cannot trust someone, *do not hire that person!* You must trust people going into the relationship! If you are a leader who feels even the slightest hesitation in accepting this point—and believe me, you have plenty of company, because I have run into hundreds, probably thousands of leaders who are skeptical about this—let me ask you to consider the following: If you do not trust your employees, do you think they will be able to pick up on that? Of course they will! And if they pick up on that lack of trust on your part, do you think they are going to find it easy to start trusting you? Of course not! So what are you doing? You are beginning this working relationship with zero trust. Where there is zero trust, *they have no reason and no motivation to want to earn your trust!* They will be too busy protecting themselves...and who can blame them? Would *you* feel safe around a boss who started out a relationship on that footing? Would you go out on a limb for that boss? Would you make sacrifices for that boss? Would you pray you could spend your career working for that person? No! Why not? Because you do not trust each other!

It *is* personal. And it is our job as leaders to respect and honor the personal relationship we have with those who are counting on us. We do that by making, and keeping, *commitments* within the relationship. And do you know what makes a commitment a commitment? *The fact that you make it to support a relationship with another human being!*

Don't Waste Your Breath

Many, many leaders do not grasp the (obvious) point: *there is no such thing as a commitment if the commitment in question is not to people and relationships.* Leaders will often say things to me like: "I am committed to quality." Or: "I am committed to making this company the best it can possibly be." Or: "I am committed to hitting our revenue target this month." When we say these things as leaders, we are wasting our breath.

What we need to be talking about is *our personal commitment to the team members who will make those outcomes possible.* If our so-called "commitment" never turns into a *relational* commitment—a commitment that supports and improves the *relationship* we have with someone who is counting on us—then that "commitment" is nothing more than hot air!

Let's assume that you are the senior leader of a company with 100 employees, and let's say that you are facing major challenges in the marketplace. Revenues are down sharply. And let's also assume that as a result of those challenges, you wake up eager to announce the following to the entire company at your weekly meeting: "I am committed to reducing our costs by 15 percent this quarter."

That is not a commitment, because it is not personal! It is manipulation!

What does it actually mean to say that you are "committed" to such a thing? Are you saying that you are personally going to ensure that all budgets across the board are simply reduced by that amount of 15 percent? That has been done, and it is always entertaining whenever it happens…but is it really the best possible way to achieve the outcome you are after? Are there going to be any practical repercussions to that across-the-board cut? Are there going to be morale implications? Is it possible you might demotivate, or even lose, some good people by following this course of action? Yes!

Do you know what another reliable way to alienate good employees would be? Micromanaging every department's budget and deciding for yourself what is an essential expense and what is not—even when you have no idea what is really going on in that department. This kind of decision predictably brings on chaos, disaffection, and a downward performance spiral—all the kinds of things that happen when leaders tell themselves things like "If I want it done right, I have to do it myself!"

Actually, if you want it done right, you want to make, reinforce, and follow through on a *relational commitment*.

The Power of Relational Commitments

Suppose you were to take a different approach. Suppose you were to gather your direct reports together and say this to them: "As you probably already know, our industry is going through some challenges right now, and a lot of companies that do what we do are struggling to keep the doors open. I want you to know that I am totally committed to you. I am committed to making sure this company, all of our employees, and each and every one of us thrives and performs up to full potential. I am committed to ensuring that we continue to deliver amazing products and services to our customers so that we can continue to have a great reputation in the marketplace. I am committed to making sure we operate according to sound financial principles. I am also committed to telling you the truth, which means I need to tell you that we are facing some budgetary pressure right now...because our sales are down nationally. So I need your help. What I am looking for is your best, most creative ideas on how we can reduce our expenses in each of your departments by 15 percent with the least possible disruption to our customers. Can I ask you to get together with your people, do some brainstorming, and meet back with me here in 48 hours so we can discuss your best ideas for doing that?"

That IS a commitment—because it is personal!

Notice how different this is from telling your people you are "committed" to reducing their budgets without their input!

In that earlier case, you were the one who is focused on a single, narrow goal—eliminating expenses company-wide. You could pretend you were qualified or even capable of doing that on your own without hurting your business, but the truth is you are just one person, even if you are a senior leader. *You could not do this on your own.*

In the *second* case, because you have reinforced and followed through on specific *relational* commitments—supporting the team and each individual in it to thrive and perform optimally, supporting your customer relationships and your company's reputation, making sound financial decisions, and telling the truth—you now have a small *army* of 200 people who are inspired by your commitments because your commitments are *to them*. Not only that—they are eager to help you *fulfill* those commitments by proposing intelligent strategies for trimming expenses without cutting quality.

Who knows? They might just come up with some ideas that you would not have!

Commitments are, by definition, to people. When you say you are "committed" to some abstract goal or concept—e.g., frugality, excellence, or being number one—you are on your own. When you make and fulfill commitments to people and relationships, you draw on the massive power of organizational and team accountability!

Relational vs. Tactical

Notice that the kinds of commitments we are talking about here are not tactical commitments; they are not the kinds of commitments we make when we say, "Yes, I will get that report done by 4:00 p.m. today" or "Yes, I will clean up the kitchen before I come to bed." Those are commitments about *things*. Those are items you check off a to-do list. The kinds of commitments I am talking about—the kinds of commitments that make Pivoting possible no matter what obstacle or challenge you are up against—go much deeper than that and have a far greater impact.

Why? Because they are about people. Accountable people are committed to people—not things! Accountable leaders are committed to making their *people* great, not to "making the company great." It is the *great people* in the company who can make the company great!

> Accountable people are committed to people—not things!

Relational commitments are all about supporting people and relationships. These are long-term commitments that make *contributions* that help everyone—leaders, followers, family members, basically any and every member of the human race—to build deeper, more meaningful relationships with the people in their life. Without strong relational commitments, tactical commitments are meaningless. They bob along on the surface of one's life and do not have any meaningful impact on what is happening down below.

There are ten key relational commitments that define accountability. I want to share these ten commitments with you now to help you to narrow your learning curve as you take on the question *What am I committed to?* Accountable people—people who emerge as leaders in their own life, regardless of whether they are considered leaders of a team or an organization—make all ten of these relational commitments. Whether they are presented in these words, in other words, or in no words at all, these ten commitments are, I believe, the beating heart of all thriving families, teams, organizations, and communities. Study them closely, and notice that these commitments are experienced at a very deep level by the people to whom they are made. Bear in mind, too, that although commitments are "no matter what," relational commitments differ from tactical commitments in that relational commitments are defined *only by our actions.* Relational commitments are not commitments because they are stated. They are commitments because they are lived. And they are lived because they are what you believe.

> Relational commitments are not commitments because they are stated. They are commitments because they are lived. And they are lived because they are what you believe.

Relational Commitment #1:
I Commit to Discover and Realize My Own Potential...and to Help Others Reach Theirs

This commitment reminds us that we cannot be our very best unless we are helping others be their very best. Fulfilling this commitment is a trait of all great leaders.

Relational Commitment #2:
I Commit to the Truth

Lying and accountability cannot coexist. When we take on this commitment, we accept that seeking and speaking truth may not always be easy, but an accountable relationship is impossible without it.

Relational Commitment #3:
I Commit to Live My Values

Your core values state your principles and your standards of behavior. Your values are based on your Source. Values are closely related to beliefs. Your values are that which is truly important to you. When you value something, you do your level best to hold on to it, and if you lose it, even for a moment, you move heaven and earth to get it back.

Relational Commitment #4:
I Commit to "It's All of Us"

When you commit to "It's all of us," you accept that you do not succeed unless the other person succeeds—and you accept that if the other person fails, you fail. This commitment starts with the people in your world and extends outward until it eventually encompasses the entire human family. It may take some time for you to get to the point where you take on the commitment at that level, but that does not change the nature of the commitment.

Relational Commitment #5:
I Commit to Embrace Faults and Failures as Well as Opportunities and Successes

Living this commitment means you embrace both your best and worst moments. You speak up about your own shortcomings, and you see discussing them as opportunities for growth. You do not judge others based on their worst moments.

Taking on this commitment means adopting the mindset of "I am not perfect, and I do not expect you to be perfect." Failure is a part of human life. We all can learn from failure. Accepting this fact reinforces our commitment to support each other's growth and development.

Relational Commitment #6:
I Commit to Sound Financial Principles

This commitment is all about stewardship and making wise decisions with our financial resources. We come to this world empty-handed. We leave it empty-handed. In between, it is our job to maintain "our" resources responsibly—including, but not limited to, financial resources.

We all have different means. That is fine. The big question here is, how do we go about making responsible financial decisions based on the realities of our own situation? How do we protect ourselves and the people who are counting on us to honor this commitment? How do we make a positive impact in our community? It is possible we may need to bring in professionals to help us with those choices. The people we trust the most can help us determine whether or not this is the case, and if so, what steps we should take.

Relational Commitment #7:
I Commit to a Safe Space

When people first hear about the seventh relational commitment, they sometimes think it is exclusively about people's physical safety. That is part of this commitment, of course, but the commitment to a safe space is incomplete if we stop there, because we have not even scratched the surface when we make sure the people around us are physically safe.

This commitment is about creating and sustaining an environment of physical, emotional, and psychological safety. Remember: what we allow in our space, we condone. When we take on this commitment, we embrace the importance of personal safety, but of much more, too: we celebrate the importance of collaboration and respectful dialogue in all our interactions. We accept that bias, discrimination, and the habit of passing judgment keep us from creating a safe place for everyone.

Relational Commitment #8:
I Commit to "My Word Is My Bond"

This commitment reminds us that what we say must align with what we do. It also reminds us that there is a difference between tactical failures (situations where we have taken on a task and we experience a breakdown in fulfilling it) and commitment failures (situations where we make a conscious choice to step aside from a relational commitment). The former is to be expected from time to time, and it is usually something we can fix on our own with quick, attentive action and good communication. The latter, however, is a sign of a bigger problem, one that needs to be addressed quickly and decisively.

Relational Commitment #9:
I Commit to Stand with You When All Hell Breaks Loose

This commitment is all about being there when people need you. There will be tough times in life. When we take on this commitment, we take on the decision to give people who have a right to count on us the support they need when they need it most, even if that is not convenient or easy.

Relational Commitment #10:
I Commit to a Good Reputation

This commitment reminds us that our actions matter—not just in the outcomes we deliver today, but in what people say about us, our organization, and our team tomorrow. If we are serious about taking on and honoring the other critical relational commitments mentioned here, then our reputation will take care of itself. If we are not serious about those commitments, then word about that will inevitably get around.

Relational Commitments: It's Personal

The one absolutely critical takeaway about relational commitments is that they are *personal*.

So for example: If you happen to be the CEO of a company, does the tenth relational commitment, the one about reputation, extend to you on a personal level? It does. Why? Well, does what people say, think, and repeat to each other about your company matter to you as an individual and to the employees who look to you for leadership? It does. So, your personal commitment to each and every one of your employees to defend, support, and expand the good reputation of the company you lead must be absolute, unwavering, and non-negotiable. It should also *not need to be spoken*. There may be times when it is appropriate and necessary for you to speak explicitly about your commitment to support the company's good reputation, of course, but notice that this commitment exists *whether or not you choose to speak about it. Your actions shout it.*

Notice, too, that it represents a commitment to *all* of the employees in your organization, *whether or not you have ever met the employee in question*. By the way, if you doubt whether it is possible to have a personal commitment to someone you have never met, I have a question for you: Would you want a first responder to have a personal commitment to you, your safety, and your well-being if you were involved in an automobile accident? I thought so.

Now let's say that you are *not* the CEO of a company. Let's say that you are a parent who does not happen to have any job that pays you a monetary salary…but you do have the important job of supporting and taking care of your family. Does the tenth relational commitment, the one about committing to a good reputation, apply to you? Absolutely! Think about it. Does what people think, say, and feel about your *family* matter? It does! Does your *family* have a reputation, a reputation that you are committed to defending, supporting, and expanding? It does! Do you have a *personal* commitment to each and every member of your family to make decisions that take the family's reputation into account and improve that reputation? I certainly hope so! Does that commitment exist even if you do not talk about it very much—or ever? Yes!

Relational commitments are always personal...because they always affect your relationship with individual human beings. If you make and honor these commitments, you are accountable. If you ignore or undermine these commitments, you are not accountable. It is that simple.

If you happen to make a decision that damages or undermines the relational commitments you have taken on, it will, by definition, damage your relationships. That is a personal impact. On the other hand, if you approach decision-making with these commitments in mind, *you are accountable.* And the quality of the relationships improves. That is a personal impact, too.

Relational Commitments: A Case Study

I would like to share one of my favorite examples from history of an accountable leader whose decisions supported all ten of these relational commitments. As the supreme commander of Allied forces in the summer of 1944, General Dwight D. Eisenhower had the personal responsibility of deciding when and where to launch the naval invasion of France, which he knew would be the largest seaborne invasion in human history. The risks connected to the massive military operation were immense, and so were the risks of postponing action.

In early June, Eisenhower's generals recommended that he launch the invasion despite adverse weather conditions. The reasoning behind the strategy they proposed was twofold: they argued that, given the bad weather, German generals were likely to be more confident that Eisenhower would not attack…and they also maintained that the logistical and security implications of continuing to keep 160,000 soldiers, sailors, and airmen in place and ready for action on a vast assortment of ships and bases were quickly growing unmanageable. "I don't like it," Eisenhower told his seniors advisors, "but we have to go."

He gave the order to invade. At the same time, he could not stop thinking about what would happen if the invasion failed. In preparation for that possible outcome, he drafted an extraordinary memo that he planned to deliver as a speech in the event that the Allied forces were repelled at Normandy. Its text read as follows:

> Our landings in the Cherbourg-Havre area have failed to gain a satisfactory foothold and I have withdrawn the troops. My decision to attack at this time and place was based upon the best information available. The troops, the air and the Navy did all that bravery and devotion to duty could do. If any blame or fault attaches to the attempt it is *mine alone*.[1]

The words "mine alone" are underlined.

As it happened, Eisenhower did not have to deliver that radio address to the world. The Normandy invasions took time, but they were a military success. Notice, though, that his first instinct was to protect the lives of as many servicemen as possible by calling off the invasion if it became obvious that it could not succeed (thereby honoring his commitment to a safe place); to defend the honor of the members of the armed forces who had trusted him with their lives (thereby honoring the commitment to protect the reputation of the soldiers and airmen under his command); and to stand up and insist that any blame or fault-finding associated with the decision to launch the attack be directed at him personally (thereby honoring the commitment to "It's all of us").

In writing that brief message, Eisenhower avoided any instinct to obscure the facts, to cast blame, or to protect himself personally. He honored his relational commitments to the utmost. Accountable leadership and accountable decision-making have seldom been displayed in such striking and vivid colors.

Everything I can uncover about this incident and about Eisenhower's career overall suggests that he was the kind of leader who leveled with people, who protected the good reputation of the institutions he served, who had the backs of those who reported to him, and who never put it on the soldiers, sailors, and airmen when there was a problem. In fact, his memo supports, directly or indirectly, all of the relational commitments at which we have been looking. It is no wonder that he did not have to deliver that radio address accepting personal responsibility for the failure of the Normandy invasion. The kind of leadership he showed produces accountability in return and inspires those on the front lines to do anything and everything in their power to ensure the mission is a success. That is what living these commitments produces.

The Ten Relational Commitments

Write this sentence in your *Pivot!* Journal:

BIG QUESTION NUMBER THREE: **WHAT AM I COMMITTED TO?**

Next, answer ALL of the following questions in your *Pivot!* Journal. Take as much time as you need to respond to them.

Exercise #1: Potential

How is the commitment to discover and realize your own potential and to help others reach theirs showing up in your life right now? How *could* it show up over the next 30 days in your relationships with family members? With those you work with? What specific changes will you make to ensure that this commitment shows up in those settings by this time next month?

Exercise #2: Truth

How is the commitment to the truth showing up in your life right now? To whom have you NOT honored this commitment? How did that happen? What can you do between now and this time next month to make sure the commitment shows up in your relationship with that person? How is the commitment to the truth showing up in your relationships with your colleagues?

Exercise #3: Values

Based on what you learned about your beliefs in Chapter 3, what are your values? How is the commitment to live your values showing up in your life right now? In what relationships have you NOT lived your values fully? What steps can you take between now and this time next month to make sure you live those values in that relationship?

Exercise #4: "It's All of Us"

How is the commitment to "It's all of us" showing up in your life right now? Where is it NOT showing up? How do you feel when someone around you is not living this commitment in regard to you? What steps can you take over the next 30 days to ensure that the people in your world know that when they win, you win...and when they lose, you lose?

Exercise #5: Faults and Failures

How is the commitment to embrace faults and failures, as well as opportunities and successes, showing up in your life right now? How did you respond the last time someone failed in your world? When was the last time you proactively shared one of your mistakes or weaknesses with someone else? If you cannot think of such a time, why is that? What steps can you take over the next 30 days to ensure that this value shows up for you at work, at home, and everywhere in between?

Exercise #6: Finances

How is the commitment to sound financial principles showing up in your life right now? Of what resources are you a steward? (Make a list.) Do you have a financial plan? If not, what steps can you take over the next 30 days to begin setting one up? How does giving show up in your financial plan? How do your financial decisions set an example for the people around you?

Exercise #7: Safe Space

How is the commitment to a safe space showing up in your life right now? Do you ever tell stories or jokes that poke fun at someone for who they are or what they believe? What have you allowed in your space that could have made it feel unsafe for others? What choices will you make differently over the next 30 days to make this commitment a daily reality in your life?

Exercise #8: "My Word Is My Bond"

How is the commitment to "My word is my bond" showing up in your life right now? Before you make a promise or commit to something, what is your thought process? In what situations do you tell people that you cannot promise something? When do you say "no"? What happens when you make a promise and then encounter an obstacle to keeping that promise that no one could have foreseen? What do you do? How will you handle this situation differently over the next 30 days?

Exercise #9: "I Stand with You"

How is the commitment to stand with you when all hell breaks loose showing up in your life right now? How do you appeal to your Source during tough times? How are you supporting others in your life when they encounter tough times? When people around you have challenges, do they turn to you? If yes, why? If no, why not? What will you do differently over the next 30 days to ensure that you are there for the people around you during challenging times?

Exercise #10: Reputation

How is the commitment to a good reputation showing up in your life right now? How is your reputation seen by others? How do you know? What do you need to change in your actions today that will impact how your reputation is perceived tomorrow? What decisions have you made over the past 30 days that had the potential to negatively impact your reputation, your family's reputation, or your organization's reputation? How will you approach those situations differently over the next 30 days?

Please do not move on to the next chapter of this book until you have completed all of this chapter's exercises and also responded to the following questions.

Take a few minutes to answer these questions briefly in your *Pivot!* Journal.

- What happens when, through your actions, the people around you come to feel that you are making and keeping the commitments identified in this chapter?
- Which specific relationships can you improve by consistently living these commitments?
- What will happen as a result of your improving those relationships?

Note

1. Dwight D. Eisenhower quoted in Eloise Lee, "Here's the Chilling Letter General Eisenhower Drafted in Case the Nazis Won on D-Day," June 6, 2012, *Business Insider*, http://www.businessinsider.com/d-day-in-case-of-failure-letter-by-general-eisenhower-2012-6.

Chapter 8

The Commitment Test

A COUPLE OF YEARS AGO, I was scheduled to give a speech in Long Beach, California. It was no accident that I was in Long Beach a day early, and as I surveyed my surroundings in my hotel room that morning I knew I was not there on vacation. I knew I was not there to sample the local restaurants. I had something else to do that day. Something important.

Weeks earlier, a good friend of mine had heard that I was scheduled to speak in Long Beach, and he had mentioned to me that while I was in the city I should visit the historic *Queen Mary* cruise ship. My friend knew that the *Queen Mary* is a beautiful reminder of an elegant, and perhaps forgotten, way of traveling the world. He also knew that the ship was now retired in Long Beach and was being used as a hotel and museum. But that was not why he had suggested I visit the ship. He made that suggestion because he knew about my family's deep ties to the *Queen Mary*.

Just hearing the ship's name from my friend's lips had brought on a strange wave of emotions. Before he had even finished speaking, I knew I had to go see it.

The talk I was supposed to give was on Sunday. I had devoted all of Saturday afternoon to the experience of boarding the *Queen Mary* and walking the same corridors its passengers would have walked back in 1939. I left my hotel and walked to the pier. As I approached, the sight of the majestic, graceful *Queen Mary* grew larger and larger and kept pulling me forward. The ship was a truly inspiring sight. I noticed that my hands were trembling and my stomach was turning somersaults.

The moment I stepped onboard, however, the trembling stopped and my stomach calmed down. It was almost as though someone had whispered in my ear, "You're safe now."

I found myself in a group of about 20 people who were obediently following a chipper, upbeat tour guide, dressed in a period uniform, like one of the crew members from the *Queen Mary*'s heyday. He shared various historical tidbits about this famous ship. One was that the *Queen Mary*, along with its sister ship the *Queen Elizabeth*, is credited with shaving between one and one and a half years off of World War II because of the number of soldiers these ships were able to transport speedily to Europe from Canada, Australia, and the United States.

What the tour guide *did not* know was that my grandfather Max and his family were on the *Queen Mary* on one of the last civilian voyages this ship made before being transitioned into a military convoy. Their voyage began on Saturday, March 4, 1939. They boarded the ship under assumed names.

My forebears were Jewish refugees from Nazi persecution. They had risked everything to make it out of Hitler's Germany and set foot on that ship while it was docked in Cherbourg, France, and they had overcome extraordinary odds in keeping their family together as they boarded the *Queen Mary* and made their way to the United States. The man who had beaten those odds and made that fateful ocean journey possible was my grandfather Max. He had risked his life multiple times to get my grandmother, my mother (then 11), her older brother, and himself onto the *Queen Mary*.

Their flight from Germany was motivated by the infamous Kristallnacht in Germany on November 9, 1938. That was the night that all around the country, windows were shattered, buildings were burned and destroyed, businesses were looted, and Jews were killed without compunction. On Kristallnacht, the German police in cities large and small had collectively turned a blind eye to a wave of vicious, violent, and deadly anti-Semitism. That bloody, chaotic night sent an ominous message to each and every member of the far-flung Jewish community in Germany: *You are not welcome here. You have no legal rights that anyone will bother to defend. And you will be treated accordingly.*

Some German Jews saw Kristallnacht as a signal that things had reached their lowest point in Germany. They may have concluded, wrongly, that the persecution could not get much worse, and that since they had survived Kristallnacht, they might find a way to simply ride out the wave of hatred sweeping Germany. Others wanted to leave but were unable to do so. I cannot imagine how I would have reacted if I had been alive at that time and place. I do know my grandfather saw Kristallnacht as the turning point. He took that dreadful night as his cue to protect his loved ones, and he started looking for ways to get his family out of Germany.

It was not easy. It took a while. It was an expensive proposition. But that was his commitment, and he followed through on it.

Initially, he was able to get only his wife and his son and daughter out of Germany and into Switzerland—not himself. They waited for him across the border. After three tries, the ordeal of wandering through a dense forest that bordered Switzerland and Germany and being shot at, and a fistfight with a suspicious SS officer from whom he somehow managed to escape, my grandfather was finally able to use a passport that he had personally forged. He succeeded in crossing the border, left Germany, and made his way to join his family in Switzerland.

Then, after significant bargaining, he was able to transport his family by train across France to Cherbourg, where in March of 1939 they boarded the *Queen Mary* and, after a long ocean voyage, finally came to safety in the United States.

That is the ship I was visiting that day in Long Beach—the ship that brought my family to safety in America and saved their lives.

Now, whenever I think about what it means to take on that Third Big Question, *What am I committed to?*, I think about my grandfather.

I look back on what he accomplished over 80 years ago, and I think, "That's what real commitment looks like."

He was committed to doing whatever he had to do to ensure the safety and well-being of his family. He was absolutely locked in on that outcome. Specifically, he was committed to *"It's all of us."* And to *stand with you when all hell breaks loose.* And to ensure that his wife and two children had the chance to *develop their full potential.*

Let me be clear about something: Plenty of good people tried and failed to make it out of Germany at around the same time my grandfather did. Maybe he got lucky. Maybe he and his family got out as part of some larger plan. I do not know why such things happen or do not happen. All I know is, for whatever reason, my grandfather and his family were able to make the crossing. That was his service. That was how he Pivoted!

My grandfather responded to horrific persecution by taking on the assumption that there was simply no alternative to fulfilling his commitments...which in his case meant finding some way to get his family to America. He was totally committed to leading them to safety and then to positioning them to achieve their fullest possible potential and live their lives in freedom. His unwavering level of commitment is why I found myself weeping quietly as I followed a group of tourists through an old cruise liner in Long Beach, California.

Was his commitment "personal"? Of course.

Are *all* commitments that really matter—*all* commitments that truly make a difference in people's lives—"personal"? Of course. This is the great test we all face as human beings, the Commitment Test. When we make a commitment, we must invest in it personally.

When I think of that ship my grandfather and his family boarded more than eight decades ago, I find myself posing some big questions about the power of commitment. For instance:

- What if we all made our commitments personal?
- What would it be like if you felt that your boss, your leader, felt that same level of commitment to you as an employee that my grandfather felt for his family?
- What would happen if the leader of your organization was just as committed to you as an individual as my grandfather was to his family?
- What if that leader was willing to be 100 percent committed to "It's all of us," to your growth as a person, and to your success as an employee?

- Why does that level of commitment have to be limited to the family?

- Why can't it be that way in a business?

- What if the leader of your organization decided there was simply no alternative to giving you what you needed to succeed?

- What if every leader of every organization took on a deep level of personal commitment to each and every person in that organization?

- What would be possible for you, for your team, and for your company, if the leader of your team was 100 percent committed to each and every one of its employees at the level my grandfather was committed to his family?

- What would *you* commit to accomplish for such a leader?

- What if you *were* that leader?

By now you know that I believe all commitments are personal. I believe that is what it means to make a commitment: to stand behind it at a personal level, in defense of a relationship, no matter what. That is the Commitment Test. My grandfather passed it. And to this day, he inspires me to become the kind of person who passes that same test, moment after moment and day after day.

Commitment is what makes life's greatest journeys possible. My grandfather knew what his journey had to be, and he committed to it fully *at the age of 50*—at a time when as a successful businessman, he might have been expecting his life to become more predictable and more driven by a comfortable routine. The world in which he lived had other ideas. That world challenged him to Pivot. And he met that challenge…through the strength of his personal commitment to my grandmother, my uncle, and my mother. Fulfilling that commitment was my grandfather's great journey.

So, what is your journey?

What is your commitment?

And to whom are you willing to make that commitment?

Epilogue

The Journey

HERE IS MY PROMISE to you: At some point in your life, you will be thrown for a loop. You will come up against an obstacle, a challenge, a difficulty you did not expect. Your life will be turned upside down, and you may even be tempted to conclude that you are living through a uniquely painful time, a time that presents unprecedented challenges, a time that is dark and dangerous and dispiriting. At any given moment, the pressures and events of the day may cause some people in your world to choose to perpetuate cycles of fear, anger, and greed. But I would remind you that human history has always delivered times like those and that even in the supposedly darkest times, some people choose instead to Pivot.

You can be one of them.

There will always be dark events. And there will always be some people—my grandfather Max, for instance—who rise above those events to make conscious choices about what they believe, what they focus on, and what they commit to. I wrote this book to help you take your rightful place as one of those people. And I would remind you that you always have a choice. You can always make choices that sustain love, compassion, and generosity in your life and the lives of those around you. You can always choose to Pivot!

Yes, your character will be tested. Some of the tests will be small, and some will be large. And each and every one of your choices, whenever you do find your character tested, will serve as the answer to these questions: *Who are you, and what do you believe?*

We always get to choose the Source of our beliefs. It may be the silent question "What would my grandfather do in this situation?" It may be the Bible, it may be the Quran, it may be the Torah, or it may be some other book that is important to you. Whatever it is, stick with it. We know that in order to be defendable, our Source and our belief system must value people and respect the rights of others. But we also know that we must choose to follow that Source once we identify it. We always have a choice about what voices and influences we are going to listen to when it comes to deciding what we really stand for…and where we draw the lines of right and wrong in our life.

When we ignore our Source and make decisions that do not align with our best selves, we make the world a darker, more dangerous place, and we make our lives smaller and more self-absorbed. On the other hand, when we choose words and actions that align with our most deeply held BELIEFS, we deepen our character, we make the world a better place, and we are better positioned to serve the larger human family. As part of that service, we can live according to our Source and build a successful business if that is what we choose to do. By the way, my experience has shown that we will build a better, stronger, and more sustainable business in the long run by living according to our Source. And remember: knowing what we really believe, and living according to our Source, is something we want to do *regardless* of whether we are currently facing a challenge in our life. We always have the opportunity to live like that.

> Knowing what we really believe, and living according to our Source, is something we want to do *regardless* of whether we are currently facing a challenge in our life. We always have the opportunity to live like that.

We always get to choose whether we are FOCUSING on things we can control or things we cannot control. When we choose to focus on that which we cannot control, we are subject to fear and we make excuses. When we choose to focus on that which we can control, we make decisions and we move forward in our lives.

We always get to choose the COMMITMENTS we will make, and honor, in our relationships. When we make commitments but fail to honor them, we damage our relationships and undermine our own sense of who we are meant to be. When we open ourselves up to making and keeping relational commitments—commitments that serve others and support our connections to people—extraordinary things begin to happen.

I believe that we will develop five critical best practices as the result of putting into daily practice the day-by-day, minute-by-minute decision to Pivot. Those best practices are:

- *Getting clarity.* Being honest with ourselves.

- *Letting go of what does not work.* Clearing out assumptions and habits that do not serve us.

- *Cultivating bravery.* It takes courage to go outside our comfort zone. We need to find ways to reward ourselves each time we do it.

- *Being consistent in execution.* This means doing the right thing, not just once, but over and over again.

- *Going back to our Source.* There will be countless pressures on us to take shortcuts and compromise what we believe. If we make a habit of returning to our Source, we will stay the course.

As I close this book, I would like to share one final, simple insight on the neglected art of Pivoting. If what you are doing brings you joy—not passing pleasure, but enduring joy—keep doing it. Once joy is your experience, you can be certain that you have aligned yourself with both your Purpose and your Mission. Keep pursuing that joy, and you will keep discovering and rediscovering what your Purpose and your Mission really are, and that is what each of us was put on earth to do. If you can continue pursuing that joy, you will find yourself with a precious opportunity: the opportunity to live out your Purpose and make a meaningful contribution and a lasting difference in the lives of others. Do that, and you will make Pivoting a way of life.

_____

_____

_____

_____

_____

_____

_____

_____

_____

_____

_____

_____

_____

_____

_____

_____

_____

_____

JOURNAL

JOURNAL

Pivot!

JOURNAL

JOURNAL

JOURNAL

JOURNAL

About the Author

SAM SILVERSTEIN is dedicated to empowering people to live accountable lives, transform the way they do business, and create a more accountable world. He helps companies create an organizational culture that prioritizes and inspires "Accountability...The Highest Form of Leadership™."

Sam is recognized internationally as a leading expert in organizational culture and accountability. He has enjoyed success as an author, speaker, and entrepreneur, and sold one of his companies to a Fortune 500 company. Sam's work with entrepreneurs, multinational companies, and government agencies has transformed organizational cultures and driven increased engagement and productivity. He is the founder of Pivot!, an online community of values-based leaders who want to move beyond self-imposed limitations by fully living their beliefs, purpose, and mission.

Sam has written numerous books, including *I Am Accountable, No More Excuses, No Matter What, The Success Model, Non-Negotiable, Making Accountable Decisions, The Accountability Circle,* and *The Lost Commandments.*

Sam Silverstein can be reached at 314-878-9252.

Book Sam Silverstein
To Speak At Your Next Event

Contact Us

Sam Silverstein, Incorporated
121 Bellington Lane
St. Louis, Missouri 63141
info@SamSilverstein.com
(314) 878-9252

To Order More Copies of
Pivot!

www.samsilverstein.com

Follow Sam

www.twitter.com/samsilverstein

www.youtube.com/samsilverstein

www.linkedin.com/in/samsilverstein

www.instagram.com/samsilverstein

www.facebook.com/silversteinsam

No More Excuses | Making Accountable Decisions | The Success Model | I Am Accountable

Other books by **SAM SILVERSTEIN** available <u>everywhere books are sold.</u> or www.SamSilverstein.com

No Matter What | The Lost Commandments | Non Negotiable | The Accountability Circle